SENCERA GREI

Mastering Retail Profits

A Comprehensive Guide for New Business Owners

PTM

PENNIES TO MILLIONS

First published by Pennies to Millions Publishing 2024

First edition

"Strategy without tactics is the slowest route to victory. Tactics without strategy is the noise before defeat."

- Sun Tzu

Contents

Preface   ii

Introduction   1

Components of Product Costing   8

Calculating Margins   18

The Power of Historical Sales Data   30

Tailoring Prices to Unique Value Proposi-
tions and...   42

Strategies for Increasing Profit Margins   53

The Ethics of Pricing   65

Marketing and Pricing   76

Pricing in the Digital Age   89

Adapting to Economic Fluctuations   101

Navigating Global Supply Chain Challenges   113

Regulatory Changes and Profit Margins   126

Emerging Trends in Retail   136

Sustainability and Pricing   142

Building Resilience and Protecting Margins   155

Conclusion   170

Resources   180

Index   183

Preface

After over 25 years as a consultant and 7 years at a fortune 500 retailer, I have witnessed hundreds of entrepreneurs launch and grow thriving businesses. Time and again, the difference between lackluster enterprises and exceptionally successful ones lies in mastery of profit margins, no matter what business your in. Yet for fledgling founders, this crucial competency often seems shrouded in mystery and complexity.

This book is my attempt to demystify retail profit margin management for aspiring retailers. Throughout decades of experience, I have distilled the fundamentals critical for maximizing earnings, optimizing operations, and securing financial stability. Within these pages, I share the precise frameworks, actionable advice, and lessons learned working alongside numerous clients. Consider this book the playbook I wish every new retail business owner possessed on day one.

Why am I so passionate about imparting this knowledge? As CEO of The Retail Concepts Company, my mission is helping entrepreneurs translate their ambitions into achievement. I firmly believe that armed with the right strategies, small businesses can become industry leaders. I have seen the transformative impact of putting proven profit-enhancing principles into practice.

Yet entrepreneurial success transcends merely enhancing bottom lines. True fulfillment stems from pursuing work you feel passionate about, creating meaningful change, and helping communities thrive. My hope is that by sharing the knowledge I've been fortunate enough to accrue, I can empower founders not only to maximize margins but also to live their definition of success.

The journey ahead will undoubtedly be challenging but profoundly rewarding. So let this book be your guide as you take the first steps towards mastering margins and unlocking your entrepreneurial potential. It is not the end all be all but its the start to understanding the beginning of a beautiful journey! The opportunities waiting are truly boundless.

Wishing you tremendous success,

Sencera Grei

Introduction

I n today's hypercompetitive retail landscape, mastering profit margins is paramount to the success and sustainability of any business. Profit margins represent the very lifeblood of a company, determining its ability to cover expenses, compensate employees, reinvest, and grow. Consequently, optimizing margins should be a top priority for retailers seeking to thrive amidst the complexities and pressures of the modern market.

This book serves as an indispensable guide to mastering this critical but often overlooked aspect of running a retail business. Through comprehensive yet digestible analysis of various components affecting profitability, readers will gain a holistic perspective of what drives margins and how to leverage this knowledge to boost their bottom line.

We will examine the current retail climate, including the rise of e-commerce, shift to data-driven operations, and focus on customer experience. By understanding the trends shaping industry dynamics, retailers can anticipate changes and capitalize on emerging opportunities. However, the intensified competition also reinforces the importance of financial precision in remaining viable.

What exactly constitutes a healthy profit margin varies greatly depending on the business model, product mix, brand positioning and other factors. Yet universally, optimizing margins entails a nuanced balancing act - pricing products to balance affordability and profit generation while simultaneously streamlining operations to curb expenses. Striking this balance requires an intricate understanding of the moving parts comprising a company's cost structure.

The Complex Composition of Costs

Imagine standing in your store, surveying the meticulously organized products lining the shelves. Every item on display represents a multitude of embedded costs - from materials and labor to rent, utilities and marketing. Comprehending this intricate cost composition is imperative to managing margins.

We will break down these elements, including:

Direct Costs:

These encompass the physical materials and effort involved in creating a product. For a clothing retailer, this includes fabric, thread and other raw materials plus labor expenses for manufacturing. Understanding how choices in materials and production impact per unit costs is essential.

Overhead Expenses:

This umbrella category encapsulates operating costs to keep the business running.

Depending on the company, these range from lease payments and utilities to payroll, insurance and marketing initiatives. While overhead costs are more indirect, they constitute a significant portion of expenditures.

Analyzing Costs Through Examples

To demonstrate the real-world implications of costs on margins, let's examine a hypothetical specialty boutique selling dresses for $100 each. The fabric and materials amount to $25 per dress, while outsourced labor adds $15. Therefore, the direct production cost is $40. However, when we account for the store's overhead expenses such as rent and divide it across units sold, it amounts to around $20 per dress.

Ultimately, the total expense for the boutique to bring each dress to market tallies $60.

With a selling price of $100, this yields a gross profit of $40 per unit and a 40% margin.

While respectable, this margin will subsequently diminish once additional costs like payroll, taxes and other operating expenses are incorporated to determine net profitability.

This example underscores the importance of comprehending both direct product costs alongside overhead expenses and how marginal differences greatly impact the bottom line at scale. As we will explore later, routinely performing these profit calculations is vital for retailers to understand their earnings potential and optimize every variable possible to expand margins.

Pricing & Profit Margins Inextricably Linked

Beyond expenses, setting optimal prices represents the other lynchpin in profit margin mastery. Price point decisions carry monumental weight, forging the gateway between revenue goals and financial realities. Prices establish expected profits while simultaneously conveying value perceptions that must resonate with target markets.

For specialty retailers concentrated in niche categories, pricing flexibility may exist to prioritize profit generation. The perceived exclusivity and quality of products can justify premium price tags. However, mass-market generalists with more price-sensitive customers often operate on thinner margins in exchange for higher volume sales.

Understanding pricing psychology among diverse customer segments is mandatory when calibrating margin expectations.

No universally ideal profit margin threshold exists. Rather, this benchmark differs based on business models, product types, brand identities and strategic goals. However, actively analyzing margins across time, departments and inventory categories allows retailers to pinpoint strengths versus improvement areas. We will explore various pricing tactics and strategies for balancing affordability with profit goals. Readers are encouraged to continually practice margin calculations using their own company data to inform pricing decisions.

Beyond Price & Costs

While foundational, calibrating prices and costs alone is insufficient to maximize profit margins. Retailers must also implement additional strategies surrounding inventory management, customer experience, technologies and operational efficiency.

Here we will explore various techniques, including:

- Leveraging historical sales data and forecasting to optimize inventory planning and avoid costly overages or shortages
- Crafting targeted marketing campaigns to increase average order values
- Building loyalty programs and personalized engagement to foster repeat business
- Diversifying product selections to appeal to wider audiences
- Investing in technologies like BI analytics, CRM platforms and automation to work smarter

Again, real-world examples will showcase how retailers have employed these tactics to significant financial benefit. When woven together, these multifaceted strategies form a comprehensive blueprint for taking command of profit margins.

A Preview of What's Ahead

As we progress chapter-by-chapter, this profit margin guide-book will equip readers with insights and tools to thrive amidst the intricacies and turbulence of retail. Key lessons include:

Components of Product Costing - Dive deep into the factors that contribute to the cost of goods sold (COGS) in retail, including direct costs like raw materials and labor, as well as overhead expenses such as rent, utilities, and marketing. Provide real-world examples to illustrate these concepts.

Calculating Margins - Teach readers how to calculate gross profit margin and net profit margin, with step-by-step instructions and examples. Emphasize the relationship between margins, pricing, and the bottom line. Include hands-on exercises for readers to practice calculating margins for their own businesses.

The Power of Historical Sales Data - Explain the importance of historical sales data in predicting future trends, optimizing inventory, and managing customer behavior insights.

Provide case studies that demonstrate how businesses have successfully used data to grow and improve their operations.

Tailoring Prices to Unique Value Propositions and Positioning - Explore how to set prices based on a business's unique value proposition, competitive landscape, and target customer segments. Discuss pricing strategies by product category, such as high-volume, low-margin vs. premium pricing. Provide examples of successful pricing strategies in various industries.

Strategies for Increasing Profit Margins - Share practical tips and tricks for reducing expenses, increasing average transaction value, building customer loyalty, diversifying product lines, and exploring new technologies and trends that can enhance profitability.

Include case studies that show how businesses have successfully implemented these strategies.

The Ethics of Pricing - Emphasize the importance of fair pricing practices and the psychology of pricing that can build trust and customer loyalty. Offer strategies for making pricing more transparent and understandable to customers, including examples of ethical pricing practices in the retail industry.

As illustrated throughout this introductory overview, managing profit margins encompasses intricate complexities and interconnected components. Fortunately, demystifying retail financials does not require advanced mathematics or statistics - merely diligence to continually analyze, assess and adjust your business's moving parts. By reading this playbook cover-to-cover, retailers will gain an indispensable education and actionable strategies to bolster their financial fitness for the long-term.

Let us begin unraveling the nuances surrounding margins to unlock your company's maximum profit potential.

Components of Product Costing

E xploring the intricacies of the retail sector, a key factor emerges as essential for success: the mastery of product costing. Precisely calculating the costs tied to each product is not just influential for profit margins, but it also forms the cornerstone of broader business achievement. Within the fiercely competitive arena of retail, decisions related to pricing, inventory control, and marketing are all deeply rooted in a thorough understanding of product costing.

Product costing is the methodical calculation of the total cost incurred in producing or acquiring a particular product. This includes accounting for all expenses related to materials, labor, and overhead involved in the production or purchase of the item. The ultimate objective of product costing is to determine the actual cost of goods sold (COGS), which is an indispensable metric for any retailer striving to achieve sustainable profitability.

To further comprehend the importance of product costing, it is necessary to understand its role in determining the COGS. The cost of goods sold represents the direct costs attributable to the production or acquisition of the products sold by a company during a specific period. By accurately assessing the COGS, businesses can establish their gross profit margin, a pivotal indicator of a company's financial health. A well-informed approach to product costing allows retailers to make strategic decisions that ultimately contribute to improved performance, higher sales, and increased profitability.

Direct costs play a significant role in determining the overall cost of products. These costs are directly associated with producing or acquiring goods and can be traced back to specific items or services. Two critical components of direct costs include raw materials and labor. To illustrate, consider a clothing retailer that sources garments from a manufacturing facility. The raw materials, such as fabrics, threads, buttons, and zippers, constitute the primary direct costs of producing the clothes. The wages paid to the workers who operate the machines, cut the fabric, sew the pieces together, and package the finished products also contribute to the direct costs.

Labor expenses may vary depending on factors such as skill level, experience, and the complexity of tasks performed by the workforce. For instance, a highly skilled tailor crafting bespoke suits would command higher wages than an entry-level worker performing basic sewing tasks. It is for retailers to accurately account for both raw materials and labor costs to achieve a precise understanding of their direct costs.

Accurately calculating direct costs is essential in ensuring profitability for retail businesses. An accurate estimation enables retailers to set appropriate product prices, generating healthy profit margins while remaining competitive. Under-estimating direct costs can lead to setting prices too low, resulting in reduced profit margins or even losses. Conversely, overestimating direct costs could cause retailers to set prices higher than necessary, potentially driving customers away to more competitively priced alternatives.

Miscalculating direct costs can also lead to ineffective inventory management decisions.

For example, underestimating the direct costs of producing a particular item might prompt a retailer to stock up on excessive quantities of that product, tying up valuable capital in unsold inventory. On the other hand, overestimating direct costs could result in insufficient stock levels, leading to lost sales opportunities when customer demand cannot be met.

A thorough understanding of direct costs, which encompasses raw materials and labor, is for retail businesses to calculate the overall cost of products accurately. By doing so, retailers can make informed pricing decisions, optimize inventory management, and ultimately bolster their profitability. In the next section, we will explore the impact of overhead expenses on product costing and discuss how different businesses have effectively managed these costs through efficient strategies.

Beyond direct costs, retail businesses must also account for overhead expenses when determining the actual cost of their products. Overhead expenses encompass all indirect costs of running a company, such as rent, utilities, and marketing. These costs are not directly linked to the production of goods but are necessary for the overall operation of the business.

To accurately determine the cost of products, retailers must allocate a portion of these overhead expenses to each item they sell. This allocation can be done using various methods, such as applying a standard percentage markup or dividing total overhead costs by the number of units produced. By doing so, retailers can ensure that they are capturing the total cost of their products, which is essential for setting appropriate prices and maintaining healthy profit margins.

In the competitive world of retail, effectively managing overhead expenses can make a significant difference in a business's profitability. A prime example of this is the warehouse club Costco, which has achieved considerable success by adopting a lean operating model focused on minimizing overhead costs. By keeping its stores simple and functional, Costco can maintain lower rent and utility expenses than more elaborate retail spaces. Additionally, the company's membership-based model allows it to generate revenue through annual fees, further reducing its reliance on high product markups to cover overhead costs. As a result, Costco can offer its customers consistently low prices while still achieving strong profit margins.

Another notable example is Zara, a fashion retailer known for its rapid inventory turnover and efficient supply chain management. By investing in state-of-the-art technology and establishing close relationships with suppliers, Zara has streamlined its production process, enabling the company to respond to market trends and minimize excess inventory quickly. This efficiency extends to managing overhead expenses, as Zara strategically locates its warehouses and distribution centers to minimize transportation costs and reduce the impact of utilities on overall product costs. Through these innovative practices, Zara has positioned itself as a leader in the fast-fashion industry, boasting impressive profitability and customer loyalty.

In sum, the effective management of overhead expenses is a critical aspect of product costing that retail businesses must pay attention to. By carefully allocating rent, utilities, and marketing expenses to their products, retailers can ensure they capture the actual cost of goods sold. Furthermore, learning from examples from successful companies like Costco and Zara, businesses can implement strategies to minimize overhead costs and improve profitability. As retail business owners refine their understanding of product costing, they will be better equipped to make informed decisions that drive success in the competitive marketplace.

Businesses often face challenges when calculating product costs in the ever-changing retail industry. One such challenge is the fluctuation of raw material prices, which can be attributed to factors like supply and demand imbalances, global economic conditions, or natural disasters. Retailers must constantly monitor these fluctuations to ensure their cost calculations remain accurate and up-to-date.

To address this issue, retailers can adopt a proactive approach by negotiating long-term contracts with suppliers to lock in stable prices for a specified period. This strategy provides a measure of predictability in the cost of goods and fosters strong relationships with suppliers, which can lead to better terms and conditions in future dealings.

Labor costs, another essential component of direct costs, are also subject to change due to minimum wage legislation, employee turnover, and productivity levels. Retailers can implement strategies to manage labor costs effectively, such as offering competitive wages, providing ongoing training to improve efficiency, and utilizing part-time or seasonal workers during peak periods. Additionally, investing in automation technologies can help reduce labor costs in the long run, allowing businesses to streamline processes and improve overall operational efficiency.

As the market evolves and new trends emerge, it becomes imperative for retailers to review and update their product costing strategies regularly. This ongoing process enables businesses to adapt to changes in the business environment, such as shifts in consumer preferences, technological advancements, or increased competition. By staying attuned to these changes, retailers can make timely adjustments to their product offerings, pricing strategies, and cost structures, thus maintaining profitability and ensuring long-term success.

Regular reviews of product costing strategies may involve benchmarking against competitors and industry standards, analyzing sales data to identify patterns, and assessing the effectiveness of current methods and tools. Moreover, engaging in continuous improvement initiatives, such as adopting lean management principles or embracing digital transformation, can significantly enhance product costing accuracy and efficiency. Ultimately, a retailer's ability to adapt and respond to changes in the market will play a role in determining its success and profitability.

Retailers must navigate various challenges when calculating product costs, including fluctuating raw material prices and labor costs. Businesses can ensure their continued growth and competitiveness by implementing strategies to mitigate these challenges and maintaining accurate cost calculations. Furthermore, it is essential for retailers to regularly review and update their product costing strategies in response to changes in the market or business environment, as this enables them to make informed decisions that drive success in the competitive retail landscape.

Accurate product costing is the cornerstone of informed pricing decisions within the retail industry. It enables businesses to establish competitive prices in the market, which are essential for attracting customers and maintaining profitability. When retailers thoroughly understand their cost structures, they can determine the optimal price points that strike a balance between covering expenses, generating profit, and appealing to consumers.

Additionally, accurate product costing allows retailers to analyze the effects of potential price adjustments on their bottom line, giving them a solid foundation for making tactical decisions. For instance, they can evaluate the feasibility of offering discounts or promotions, assess the impact of seasonal fluctuations in demand, or gauge the consequences of matching competitor prices. In this way, well-informed pricing decisions depend on a retailer's ability to calculate and monitor product costs precisely.

To ensure accuracy in product costing, retailers should consider implementing practical tips and techniques that streamline the process and enhance overall efficiency. One such approach is to adopt cost accounting systems, which provide a structured method for tracking and allocating product-related expenses. These systems facilitate the identification of direct costs, overhead expenses, and other relevant factors, thus aiding retailers in determining the actual cost of goods sold.

Another helpful technique is to utilize software tools designed specifically for product costing and inventory management. These tools offer various features like automated calculations, real-time data updates, and customizable reporting options. Moreover, they can be integrated with point-of-sale (POS) systems and other business applications, creating a seamless flow of information across various operational areas. By employing these advanced technologies, retailers can enhance the accuracy of their product costing processes while also gaining valuable insights into their overall business performance.

Mastering product costing is critical for retailers seeking to make informed pricing decisions and maintain a competitive edge in the market. By adopting cost accounting systems and harnessing the power of software tools, businesses can accurately calculate and track their product costs, ultimately leading to improved profitability and sustained success.

In addition to the aforementioned practical tips and techniques, retailers can also consider outsourcing certain aspects of product costing. By enlisting the help of external consultants or specialized services, businesses can benefit from expert advice and insights explicitly tailored to their unique operational needs.

One key advantage of outsourcing product costing tasks lies in the wealth of experience and specialized knowledge that consultants bring. These professionals have likely worked with diverse businesses and industries, allowing them to draw upon a vast repository of best practices and strategies. As a result, retail business owners can expect to receive relevant and up-to-date guidance, ensuring that their product costing efforts remain aligned with current market trends and industry standards.

Moreover, outsourcing can prove particularly beneficial for smaller retailers or those with limited resources, as it enables them to access high-quality expertise without investing heavily in hiring full-time staff or purchasing expensive software tools. By partnering with specialized service providers, these businesses can focus on their core competencies while leaving the complexities of product costing to the experts.

As we have discussed, various strategies can aid retailers in enhancing their product costing processes, such as implementing cost accounting systems, utilizing software tools, and outsourcing specific tasks to external consultants or specialized services.

Retail business owners are encouraged to apply the knowledge gained from this chapter to their enterprises, tailoring the approaches and techniques to suit their specific needs and circumstances.

By prioritizing accuracy and efficiency in product costing, retailers can pave the way for improved profitability, better decision-making, and, ultimately, sustained success in today's dynamic and ever-evolving business landscape.

Calculating Margins

I n retail, calculating and understanding profit margins is vital for any business owner or manager. Maximizing profitability is making informed pricing decisions based on accurate margin calculations. In this chapter, we will explore the significance of gross profit margin and net profit margin, two key financial indicators that play a role in evaluating and optimizing the overall financial health of a retail enterprise.

Gross profit margin can be defined as a measure of the profitability of individual products or services offered by a retailer. It is expressed as a percentage and represents the difference between the cost of goods sold (COGS) and the selling price of those goods.

By analyzing the gross profit margin, retailers can gain valuable insights into the efficiency of their operations, product pricing, and overall revenue generation.

On the other hand, net profit margin takes a more holistic approach, examining the overall profitability of the entire business after accounting for all expenses, including overheads such as rent, utilities, marketing, and other costs not directly related to the production or purchase of goods. This comprehensive view enables retailers to understand their business's financial performance better, providing a deeper understanding of their profitability dynamics.

Both gross profit margin and net profit margin are essential tools for evaluating the financial health of a retail business. Not only do they offer valuable insights into the effectiveness of pricing strategies, but they also shed light on the operational efficiency and cost structures at play. By mastering these calculations and understanding their implications, retailers can make well-informed decisions leading to increased profitability and long-term success.

Calculating gross profit margin is a fundamental skill that retailers must master to make informed pricing decisions and optimize the profitability of their products or services.

We provide step-by-step instructions for this essential calculation and a hypothetical example to illustrate the process.

Step 1: Determine your total revenue

Total revenue refers to the money generated from selling your products or services. This figure can be obtained from your sales records or accounting system. For our hypothetical example, let's assume a retailer has sold 100 product units at $50 each, resulting in a total revenue of $5,000.

Step 2: Calculate the cost of goods sold (COGS)

The COGS is the sum of all direct costs associated with producing or acquiring the products you sell. This includes raw materials, labor, and other expenses directly tied to producing or procuring goods. In our example, let's say the retailer spends $20 per unit on raw materials, $10 per unit on labor, and $5 per unit on additional direct costs, totaling $35 per unit.

Step 3: Subtract COGS from total revenue

To find the gross profit, subtract the COGS from the total revenue. In our example, the retailer's COGS for the 100 units would be $35 x 100 = $3,500. Subtracting this from the total income ($5,000 − $3,500), we get a gross profit of $1,500.

Step 4: Divide the gross profit by the total revenue

Finally, divide the gross profit by the total revenue to find the gross profit margin. In our example, this would be $1,500 ÷ $5,000, resulting in a gross profit margin of 0.3, or 30%.

Understanding COGS and its components is for accurately calculating gross profit margin and making informed product pricing and cost structure decisions. The elements of COGS can vary depending on the nature of your retail business, but typically include:

1. Raw materials are the primary inputs required to produce or assemble the products you sell. For example, a furniture retailer must consider the cost of wood, fabric, and hardware when calculating COGS.

2. Labor includes the wages, salaries, and benefits paid to employees directly involved in producing or procuring goods. In our hypothetical example, labor accounted for $10 per unit.

3. Other direct costs are any additional expenses directly attributed to producing or acquiring goods. Examples include shipping fees, import/export duties, and equipment rental.

By carefully examining the components of COGS, retailers can identify areas where cost structures may be improved to increase gross profit margin. For instance, a clothing retailer might find that sourcing raw materials from a more affordable supplier or investing in automation to reduce labor costs could significantly impact its profitability.

In summary, understanding how to calculate gross profit margin and recognizing the impact of COGS components on this metric is essential for retailers seeking to maximize profitability and make informed pricing decisions. As you refine your calculations, you'll be better equipped to optimize your business's financial performance and long-term success.

To ensure the accuracy and reliability of the gross profit margin calculation, it is essential to diligently track and record the cost of goods sold (COGS). This requires a systematic approach to gathering and organizing data related to the various components of COGS, such as raw materials, labor, and other direct expenses associated with production or procurement.

One practical method for maintaining accurate records is to develop a detailed inventory system. This should include information on the quantity and cost of raw materials, work-in-progress, and finished goods. By regularly updating this system, retailers can closely monitor cost fluctuations and make informed pricing and inventory management decisions.

Additionally, tracking expenses related to production or procurement can provide valuable insights into areas where cost optimization may be possible. For instance, by monitoring shipping fees or import/export duties, retailers can identify opportunities to negotiate better rates or find alternative suppliers that offer more competitive pricing.

Having explored the importance of accurately recording COGS, let us now transition to another critical financial metric: net profit margin. Unlike gross profit margin, which focuses solely on the profitability of individual products or services, net profit margin provides a more comprehensive view of a business's overall financial health. This metric considers the direct costs of producing or acquiring goods and all other expenses, including overhead costs like rent, utilities, and marketing.

To calculate the net profit margin, subtract all expenses from the gross profit. Then, divide the result by the total revenue. Let's illustrate this with a hypothetical example:

Suppose a retailer has a total revenue of $100,000, a gross profit of $60,000, and overhead expenses totaling $30,000. The net profit margin calculation would be as follows:

Net Profit Margin = (Gross Profit - Total Expenses) / Total Revenue

= ($60,000 - $30,000) / $100,000

= $30,000 / $100,000

= 0.3 or 30%

In this example, the retailer's net profit margin is 30%, indicating that, after accounting for all expenses, the business retains 30% of its total revenue as profit.

By understanding gross and net profit margins, retailers can gain a holistic perspective on their financial performance and make informed pricing, inventory management, and cost optimization decisions. This knowledge empowers them to strike the ideal balance between profitability and competitiveness, ultimately contributing to the long-term success of their businesses.

Calculating net profit margin requires a comprehensive understanding of all expenses involved in running a retail business. It is to account for fixed costs, such as rent and utilities, and variable costs, such as marketing and inventory procurement. By considering these expenses in the calculation, retailers can obtain a more accurate picture of their business's profitability. This awareness enables them to identify areas where cost optimization may be necessary to improve the bottom line.

High overhead expenses can significantly impact the net profit margin, representing a large portion of the total costs that must be deducted from gross profit. For instance, a business with a high rent expense may need to help maintain a healthy net profit margin, even if its gross profit margin is substantial. In such cases, it becomes essential for retailers to explore opportunities for reducing overhead costs, streamlining operations, or increasing efficiency.

To calculate the net profit margin, follow these step-by-step instructions:

1. Gather data on all expenses: Compile a detailed list of all fixed and variable costs associated with running the retail business. Ensure that all expenses, such as rent, utilities, payroll, marketing, and inventory procurement, are accounted for.

2. Calculate gross profit: As previously discussed, subtract the cost of goods sold (COGS) from the total revenue to arrive at the gross profit.

3. Subtract total expenses from gross profit: Deduct the sum of all fixed and variable costs from the gross profit to determine the net profit.

4. Divide net profit by total revenue: Divide the net profit by the total revenue and multiply the result by 100 to express the net profit margin as a percentage.

Consider this real-world example to demonstrate the calculation:

A clothing retailer has a total revenue of $200,000, a COGS of $80,000, and the following expenses:

- Rent: $20,000

- Utilities: $5,000

- Payroll: $50,000

- Marketing: $10,000

- Inventory Procurement: $15,000

First, calculate the gross profit:

Gross Profit = Total Revenue - COGS

= $200,000 - $80,000

= $120,000

Next, calculate the net profit:

Net Profit = Gross Profit - Total Expenses

= $120,000 - ($20,000 + $5,000 + $50,000 + $10,000 + $15,000)

= $120,000 - $100,000

= $20,000

Finally, calculate the net profit margin:

Net Profit Margin = (Net Profit / Total Revenue) x 100

= ($20,000 / $200,000) x 100

= 0.1 x 100

= 10%

In this example, the clothing retailer's net profit margin is 10%, which indicates that after accounting for all expenses, the business retains 10% of its total revenue as profit.

By regularly calculating and analyzing gross and net profit margins, retailers can make informed pricing, inventory management, and cost optimization decisions. This process enables them to maintain a balance between profitability and competitiveness in the market, ultimately contributing to the long-term success of their businesses.

Understanding the relationship between margins, pricing, and the bottom line is critical to successful retail management. Grasping profit margins enables retailers to make informed pricing decisions that balance profitability and competitiveness. To illustrate the impact of pricing on profit margins and overall financial performance, let us consider the following example:

A local grocery store sells apples for $1 each and has a cost of goods sold (COGS) of $0.60 per apple. This results in a gross profit margin of 40% (($1 - $0.60) / $1). However, the store owner discovers that a nearby competitor sells apples for $0.90 each. To remain competitive, the store owner is considering lowering the price of apples to $0.95 each.

At this new price, the gross profit margin decreases to 36.8% (($0.95 - $0.60) / $0.95), which may lead to a reduced net profit margin if other expenses remain constant. While the lower price may attract more customers, it is essential for the retailer to carefully evaluate whether the increased sales volume will offset the decreased gross profit margin. By understanding the relationship between pricing and profit margins, retailers can make informed decisions that contribute to maximizing the bottom line.

Hands-on exercises are included throughout the chapter to engage readers further and allow them to apply what they've learned. These exercises provide sample scenarios or hypothetical situations where readers can practice calculating their businesses' gross and net profit margins. For example:

Exercise 1: A toy store has a total revenue of $150,000 and a COGS of $90,000. Calculate the gross profit margin.

Exercise 2: Using the information from Exercise 1, assume the toy store has the following expenses:

- Rent: $15,000

- Utilities: $3,000

- Payroll: $40,000

- Marketing: $7,000

Calculate the net profit margin.

These exercises encourage readers to analyze pricing strategies and cost structures to see how they impact profit margins. By engaging in these hands-on activities, readers can gain a deeper understanding of the concepts discussed and apply them to their retail businesses effectively. As retailers continue to analyze and refine their margin calculations, they will be better equipped to make informed pricing decisions that maximize profitability while maintaining competitiveness in the market.

The key points covered in this chapter have emphasized the vital role of calculating margins in retail businesses. We have explored the concepts of gross and net profit margin and their significance in evaluating a business's financial health. By understanding these important metrics, retailers can make informed pricing decisions that balance profitability and competitiveness.

As readers engage with hands-on exercises throughout the chapter, they will develop a firmer grasp of margin calculations and their impact on the bottom line. This practice will enable them to analyze different pricing strategies and cost structures effectively, ultimately maximizing profitability in their businesses.

With the foundation laid in this chapter, we now transition to our next topic, which builds upon these fundamental concepts and delves into inventory management strategies for retail businesses. As the journey through the world of retail profitability continues, readers will learn how efficient inventory management can further enhance their margins, optimize cash flow, and promote overall financial success. Stay tuned for an in-depth exploration of various techniques and best practices for managing inventory and ensuring seamless integration with the margin management principles discussed in this chapter.

The Power of Historical Sales Data

As we embark on this retail journey, it is to understand the significance of historical sales data. This information is a treasure trove of business insights, enabling them to make informed decisions and optimize their operations. Companies can uncover patterns and trends that ultimately contribute to their success in an ever-changing marketplace by examining past sales performance.

Historical sales data encompasses various indicators, each with unique potential to inform strategic decision-making. These benefits include predicting future trends, optimizing inventory levels, and gaining insights into customer behavior. Let's take a closer look at how each factor plays a role in enhancing business performance.

Predicting future trends is one of the most valuable outcomes of examining historical sales data. By identifying patterns from previous months or years, businesses can anticipate market fluctuations and adapt their strategies accordingly. This foresight allows retailers to stay ahead of their competition and capitalize on emerging opportunities. For instance, they may introduce new products or services based on the predicted demand, thus maximizing their revenue potential.

Optimizing inventory is another key advantage of harnessing historical sales data. Retailers are constantly seeking ways to balance stocking enough items to meet customer demand while minimizing the costs associated with excess inventory.

Analyzing past sales figures can help businesses identify fast-moving products, allowing them to allocate resources efficiently and avoid stockouts. Conversely, slow-selling items can be placed and managed appropriately to reduce carrying costs and wastage.

Lastly, historical sales data provides invaluable insights into customer behavior. By understanding their customers' preferences, buying patterns, and loyalty, businesses can tailor marketing efforts to resonate more effectively with their target audience. This personalized approach can increase customer satisfaction, repeat purchases, and lifetime value.

Historical sales data offers a wealth of benefits for businesses operating in the retail industry. By leveraging this information, companies can make data-driven decisions that improve operational efficiency, enhance customer experience, and increase profitability.

As we explore the intricacies of retail success, remember that historical sales data is a fundamental tool in achieving long-term growth and sustainability.

To further illustrate the power of historical sales data in action, let us examine a case study involving a mid-sized retail business specializing in apparel and accessories. This particular business faced challenges with inventory management, fluctuating customer demand, and an inability to foresee emerging trends in the market.

To address these issues, the business decided to take advantage of its existing sales records and comprehensively analyze historical data. They began by organizing their sales information into categories such as product type, price range, and customer demographic. This gave a clearer understanding of which products were performing well, which items were lagging, and the specific groups of customers that made up their target audience.

The first strategy employed by the business was a thorough examination of product performance based on historical sales data. By identifying the top-selling items and comparing them against slower-moving inventory, they could make informed decisions about which products to promote, discontinue, or adjust pricing. This led to a more efficient allocation of resources and reduced carrying costs associated with excess stock.

Another technique utilized by the business involved analyzing seasonal trends within their historical sales data. By recognizing patterns related to the time of year, they were better equipped to predict fluctuations in customer demand and adjust their inventory levels accordingly. This proactive approach helped prevent stockouts during periods of increased demand while also preventing overstocking during quieter months.

As a result of their data-driven decision-making, the business experienced several positive outcomes. Their inventory management improved significantly, lowering carrying costs and increasing cash flow. Furthermore, by identifying and capitalizing on emerging trends in customer preferences, they were able to stay ahead of the competition and boost overall sales figures.

In summary, this case study demonstrates the significant impact that historical sales data can have on a retail business's operations. By employing specific strategies and techniques to analyze past sales records, companies can unlock valuable insights that drive informed decision-making, optimize inventory management, and improve profitability.

A deeper understanding of historical sales data can be achieved by examining various data types businesses often have at their disposal. One such type is sales volume, which refers to the total number of items sold during a specific period. Analyzing sales volume can reveal patterns and trends in customer demand, helping businesses make informed decisions on production levels and marketing efforts.

Product performance is another essential aspect of historical sales data. Businesses can identify their best-sellers and underperforming items by comparing the sales data of different products. This information can then be used to optimize product offerings, pricing strategies, and promotional campaigns to drive higher sales.

In addition to sales volume and product performance, customer demographics are in understanding historical sales data. Demographic data may include age, gender, location, and income level, among other factors. This information can help retailers tailor their marketing and advertising efforts to better resonate with their target audience, ultimately increasing customer satisfaction and loyalty.

Finally, seasonal trends should be noticed when analyzing historical sales data. Seasonal fluctuations in sales can provide valuable insight into customer buying habits and preferences during specific times of the year. Retailers can use this information to plan inventory levels, promotional campaigns, and staffing requirements, ensuring they are prepared to meet customer demand during peak periods.

Businesses can utilize various tools and software to effectively collect and organize historical sales data. Data analytics tools, for instance, can help businesses process and analyze large volumes of raw sales data, revealing hidden patterns and trends that might otherwise go unnoticed. Some popular data analytics tools include Microsoft Excel, Tableau, and Google Analytics, which offer a range of features suited to different business needs.

Point-of-sale (POS) systems are another valuable resource for collecting and organizing historical sales data. These systems facilitate transactions and keep track of necessary sales data such as item quantities, prices, and customer details. By integrating a POS system with inventory and customer relationship management (CRM) software, businesses can gain an even more comprehensive view of their sales performance.

CRM software, like Salesforce or HubSpot, allows businesses to store, manage, and analyze customer data in a centralized location. By combining this information with historical sales data, retailers can better understand customer preferences, buying patterns, and loyalty. This knowledge can create personalized marketing campaigns and targeted promotions that resonate with customers individually.

Understanding the various types of historical sales data—sales volume, product performance, customer demographics, and seasonal trends—is key to unlocking valuable insights for any retail business. By employing data analytics tools, point-of-sale systems, and customer relationship management software, companies can collect, organize, and analyze this data effectively, leading to informed decision-making processes that drive growth and profitability.

In the rapidly changing retail industry landscape, staying ahead of the curve is for businesses to thrive. One key strategy that can help retailers navigate this uncertain terrain is leveraging historical sales data to predict future trends. By identifying patterns and analyzing market trends, businesses can forecast demand and make data-driven decisions to propel them forward.

For instance, a retailer might notice that the sales volume of a particular product tends to spike during specific months or seasons. By recognizing this trend, they can adjust their inventory levels accordingly, ensuring they have enough stock to meet demand during peak periods. Moreover, businesses can also analyze customer demographics and preferences, enabling them to tailor their marketing campaigns and promotions to appeal to their target audience more effectively.

At the heart of this predictive approach lies the importance of historical data analysis.

Retailers must delve into their past sales records and extract valuable insights from various metrics such as sales volume, product performance, customer demographics, and seasonal trends. These insights serve as a roadmap for anticipating consumer behavior, market shifts, and emerging opportunities.

One exemplary case study demonstrating the power of historical sales data is a mid-sized clothing retailer that faced challenges in managing its inventory and pricing strategies. Despite having a loyal customer base, the business struggled with overstocked items and fluctuating sales numbers. The retailer recognized their current approach was unsustainable and turned to historical sales data to improve its operations.

The first step they took was to analyze their past sales records comprehensively. By examining factors such as product performance, seasonal trends, and customer preferences, the retailer was able to identify patterns and areas for improvement. For example, they discovered that certain clothing styles needed more consistent performance, leading to high carrying costs and wasted storage space. As a result, they decided to discontinue these items and focus on their best-selling products.

Additionally, the retailer noticed that some items sold particularly well during specific seasons or events, such as holiday sales or back-to-school promotions. Armed with this knowledge, they adjusted their inventory levels and pricing strategies to capitalize on these periods of increased demand. Through targeted promotions and data-driven inventory management, the retailer was able to reduce its carrying costs, minimize overstock issues, and ultimately boost its overall profitability.

In summary, historical sales data is a powerful tool for businesses seeking to predict future trends in the retail industry and make informed decisions about inventory management and pricing strategies. By identifying patterns, analyzing market trends, and forecasting demand based on historical data analysis, retailers can stay one step ahead of the competition and ensure their long-term success in the ever-evolving world of retail.

The business in question implemented a series of specific steps to optimize its inventory based on historical sales data. First, they analyzed their past sales records in-depth, examining variables such as product turnover rates, customer demographics, and purchase frequency. This allowed them to identify patterns that could be used to inform their inventory management strategies.

Next, the business employed forecasting techniques to predict future demand for individual products. By comparing historical sales trends with current market conditions, they could anticipate which items would likely experience increased or decreased demand in upcoming months. This foresight enabled the company to adjust its inventory levels accordingly, ensuring that popular products remained well-stocked while minimizing the risk of overstocking slow-selling items.

Moreover, the business used this data-driven approach to reduce carrying costs associated with excess inventory. By keeping a close eye on the performance of each product and adjusting stock levels based on historical trends, they maintained an efficient inventory system that minimized storage expenses and reduced the need for costly clearance sales.

Historical sales data plays a role in managing customer behavior insights. Businesses can analyze this information better to understand customer preferences, buying patterns, and loyalty. For instance, by examining which products are frequently purchased together, companies can create tailored marketing campaigns that promote complementary items, increasing the likelihood of upselling and cross-selling.

Analyzing historical sales data also allows businesses to identify their most loyal customers. This knowledge can be leveraged to create targeted reward programs or special offers to encourage repeat business and foster long-term relationships with these valuable patrons.

For example, a retail business used historical sales data to personalize its marketing efforts. They discovered that a specific segment of their customer base consistently purchased high-end, luxury items. To cater to these customers, the retailer developed tailored email campaigns highlighting new premium products and offering exclusive discounts on luxury goods. As a result, the business saw an increase in sales among this target demographic, further validating the power of historical sales data in shaping effective marketing strategies.

Historical sales data is essential for businesses seeking to optimize their inventory management and gain valuable insights into customer behavior. By analyzing past trends, forecasting demand, and understanding customer preferences, companies can make informed decisions that ultimately lead to increased efficiency, reduced carrying costs, and a more personalized customer experience.

To ensure that businesses reap the full benefits of historical sales data, following certain best practices for effective inventory management is . One vital practice involves regularly analyzing and updating data. By consistently reviewing historical information, businesses can stay up-to-date with emerging trends, adjusting their strategies accordingly. For instance, suppose a retailer notices a sudden increase in demand for a particular product. In that case, they can quickly change their inventory levels to prevent stockouts and capitalize on the trend.

Setting inventory turnover goals is another essential practice for optimizing inventory management. Inventory turnover measures how many times a company sells through its entire inventory within a given period. High inventory turnover indicates that products are selling well and not sitting on shelves for extended periods. Businesses can monitor their performance and adjust as needed by setting specific turnover targets. For example, if a company's goal is to achieve an inventory turnover rate of 6 but currently at a rate of 4, they may need to reassess their purchasing or pricing strategies.

Implementing automated inventory management systems is also essential for maximizing the potential of historical sales data. These systems can streamline collecting, organizing, and analyzing data, allowing businesses to make informed decisions more efficiently. Automated inventory management solutions often integrate with point-of-sale systems and customer relationship management software, providing a comprehensive view of sales history and customer behavior. This holistic approach enables businesses to optimize inventory levels and more effectively cater to customer preferences.

In summary, historical sales data is an invaluable asset for businesses in the retail industry. By leveraging this information, companies can predict future trends, optimize inventory management, and gain insights into customer behavior. The key to unlocking the potential of historical sales data lies in adhering to best practices, such as regularly updating data, setting inventory turnover goals, and implementing automated inventory management systems.

By embracing data-driven decision-making, businesses can make informed choices that increase efficiency, reduce carrying costs, and enhance customer experience. As the retail landscape continues to evolve, harnessing the power of historical sales data will become increasingly important for businesses seeking to thrive and adapt in a competitive market.

Industry publications, such as the Harvard Business Review, frequently feature articles that explore the latest trends and innovations in retail data analytics. These articles often showcase successful case studies, providing valuable insights into how other businesses have leveraged historical sales data to improve their operations.

Online resources, including webinars and online courses, can also be invaluable tools for learning more about retail data analysis. Platforms like Coursera and edX offer a wide range of classes taught by experts in the field, covering topics such as data visualization, predictive analytics, and machine learning.

As we close this chapter, it's important to remember that the journey toward mastering the use of historical sales data in retail is an ongoing process. The retail landscape is ever-changing, and staying informed about the latest developments in data analytics will be for maintaining a competitive advantage.

In the upcoming chapter, we will explore a new area of focus: customer experience. By understanding the importance of delivering exceptional customer experiences, businesses can create lasting relationships with their most valuable asset - their customers. We will examine strategies for developing personalized marketing initiatives, creating memorable in-store experiences, and leveraging technology to connect with consumers meaningfully.

The next chapter promises to be an eye-opening exploration of how businesses can thrive by placing customers at the heart of their operations. Stay tuned, and prepare to gain a deeper understanding of the role customer experience plays in the success of any retail business.

Tailoring Prices to Unique Value Propositions and Positioning

I n the business world, pricing is a critical factor that can make or break a company's success. Crafting the perfect price for a product or service requires careful consideration of a business's unique value proposition, understanding the competitive landscape, and insights into target customer segments. With this foundation established, companies can explore different pricing strategies tailored to their specific product categories, ensuring their offerings are both appealing to customers and profitable.

Two distinct pricing strategies that have gained significant attention in recent years are high-volume, low-margin, and premium pricing. Both methods present advantages and challenges, but when executed effectively, they can lead to impressive results in their respective market segments.

High-volume, low-margin pricing, as its name suggests, involves setting prices at a relatively low level to encourage a large volume of sales. This strategy is particularly effective for businesses offering products or services with low production costs, as it allows them to generate significant revenue even with small profit margins per unit. The key to success with high-volume, low-margin pricing lies in striking the right balance between affordability and profitability; setting prices too low can result in insufficient profits, while putting them too high may deter potential customers and limit sales volume.

On the other hand, premium pricing adopts a different approach. Companies employing this strategy position their products or services as luxury or high-end offerings, commanding higher prices than their competitors. This method is most suitable for businesses with products or services that boast unique features, superior quality, or exceptional branding. By charging a premium price, these companies can cater to specific customer segments willing to pay more for a perceived increase in value.

Despite their differences, high-volume, low-margin, and premium pricing share a common goal: maximizing profitability through strategic price setting. To achieve this goal, businesses must carefully consider the product categories and target markets they serve, ensuring that their chosen pricing strategy aligns with their customers' unique characteristics and preferences. By doing so, companies can effectively tailor their prices to capitalize on their competitive advantages and secure a strong position in the market.

To better understand the application of high-volume, low-margin pricing strategies in real-world businesses, consider the example of Walmart. This retail giant has built its empire on offering a wide range of products at unbeatable low prices. By leveraging economies of scale and cost-efficient supply chain management, Walmart can maintain low operating costs and pass these savings onto consumers through competitive prices.

Moreover, Walmart employs aggressive marketing campaigns to attract a large customer base, emphasizing its daily commitment to providing low prices. This approach enables the company to generate substantial revenue despite the low-profit margins on individual items. As a result, Walmart has established itself as a dominant player in the retail industry, attracting customers who prioritize affordability and value for money.

Turning our attention to premium pricing strategies, one prime example is the luxury automobile industry. Brands like BMW, Mercedes-Benz, and Audi have successfully positioned themselves as purveyors of exceptional quality, performance, and style.

These automakers command higher prices than their competitors by offering vehicles with advanced features, superior craftsmanship, and a distinct brand identity that appeals to discerning consumers.

These luxury car manufacturers invest heavily in research and development, ensuring their vehicles consistently incorporate cutting-edge technology and design elements.

This commitment to innovation and excellence allows them to justify their premium prices. Consequently, these brands have cultivated a loyal following among affluent customers willing to pay more for the perceived increase in value associated with owning a high-end automobile.

In both cases – Walmart's high-volume, low-margin pricing and luxury automakers' premium pricing – the respective companies have tailored their pricing strategies to align with their target markets' unique characteristics and preferences. By understanding their customers' specific needs and desires, these businesses have been able to implement pricing approaches that maximize profitability while reinforcing their market position.

A company's value proposition is a critical foundation for establishing pricing strategies.

A strong value proposition is akin to a compass, guiding businesses toward the correct market position and enabling them to differentiate themselves from competitors. With this in mind, it becomes essential to explore the concept of value proposition and its indispensable role in setting prices.

A value proposition is the unique combination of features, benefits, and experiences a business offers its customers. It is the very reason why customers would choose one company over another. Identifying a business's unique value proposition requires careful examination of the product or service being offered and an understanding of the target market's needs and preferences. By aligning these factors, businesses can craft a compelling value proposition that differentiates them from their competition.

Consider the example of Apple Inc., a technology giant known for its innovative products and premium pricing. The company's value proposition revolves around cutting-edge design, user-friendly interfaces, and seamless device integration. By offering a high-quality, cohesive ecosystem, Apple has successfully differentiated itself from competitors and managed to command premium prices for its products. As a result, the brand has become synonymous with luxury, innovation, and reliability, catering to a specific customer segment that values these attributes.

Another example showcasing the power of a well-defined value proposition is Trader Joe's, a famous American grocery chain. Unlike traditional supermarkets, Trader Joe's offers a curated selection of high-quality, unique, and often organic products at competitive prices. Their value proposition lies in providing a distinctive shopping experience with friendly staff, exclusive private-label items, and a loyal customer base.

By tailoring their prices based on their value proposition and market positioning, Trader Joe's has carved out a niche within the intensely competitive grocery industry and remains a favorite among discerning buyers who appreciate quality, variety, and affordable prices.

Both Apple and Trader Joe's exemplify how businesses can successfully tailor their prices based on their unique value proposition. By understanding the needs and preferences of their target customers, these companies have positioned themselves strategically in the market, leveraging their pricing strategies to enhance profitability and strengthen their competitive advantage. This approach demonstrates that a well-crafted value proposition not only guides pricing decisions but also serves as a factor in determining a business's overall success.

Understanding the competitive landscape is paramount when setting product or service prices. An accurate assessment of competitors' offerings, pricing strategies, and market positioning enables businesses to make informed decisions on differentiating themselves and attracting their target customers.

A thorough competitor analysis is one effective way to gain insights into the competitive landscape. This process involves identifying direct and indirect competitors, examining their product catalogs, scrutinizing their pricing structures, and evaluating their market positioning. By doing so, businesses can uncover potential gaps in the market and opportunities to outshine competitors by offering unique value propositions and tailored pricing.

For instance, a new entrant in the organic food industry might observe that established players primarily focus on premium pricing due to the high costs associated with organic farming. However, through careful analysis, the newcomer identifies an untapped segment of budget-conscious consumers who are increasingly concerned about the environmental impact of conventional farming practices. By forging partnerships with local organic farmers and leveraging economies of scale, the new entrant adopts a competitive pricing structure that appeals to this specific customer segment, thereby carving out a unique niche in the market.

This example highlights the importance of understanding target customer segments and tailoring prices to cater to their needs and preferences. Identifying these segments requires a deep understanding of the market demographics, psychographics, and behavior patterns. For example, a luxury fashion brand might identify its target customer segment as affluent, fashion-forward individuals prioritizing exclusivity and craftsmanship over cost considerations. On the other hand, a budget airline might cater to cost-conscious travelers who prioritize affordability and convenience above all else.

Once businesses have identified their target customer segments, they can tailor their pricing strategies accordingly. In the case of luxury fashion brands, adopting a premium pricing strategy reinforces the brand's positioning as exclusive and high-quality, appealing to their target customers' desire for distinctive, well-crafted products.

Conversely, the budget airline's low-margin, high-volume pricing strategy aligns with the needs of its target customers, who prioritize affordability and accessibility.

When setting prices, understanding the competitive landscape and target customer segments is for businesses. By conducting competitor analysis and identifying gaps in the market, companies can tailor their pricing strategies to cater to specific customer needs and preferences, ensuring a more decisive competitive advantage and tremendous overall success.

To further illustrate the impact of tailored pricing strategies, let us examine a few examples of businesses that have successfully targeted specific customer segments through innovative pricing approaches.

Consider an online software company offering a subscription-based service. This business targets multiple customer segments, such as freelancers, small businesses, and large enterprises, by providing tiered pricing plans with varying features and benefits. By offering tailored plans, the software company can effectively cater to the distinct needs of each customer segment while maximizing its revenue potential.

Moreover, the business may provide personalized pricing options for specific clients based on their usage patterns or unique requirements, fostering loyalty and long-term relationships.

Another notable example is a telecommunications company that employs bundling strategies to attract and retain customers. By combining various products and services, such as mobile plans, internet packages, and entertainment subscriptions, the company can create value-added offerings that cater to the diverse preferences of its target audience. This approach not only helps attract new customers but also encourages existing ones to upgrade their plans or add more services, ultimately resulting in increased profitability for the business.

However, businesses must be mindful of several challenges and considerations when implementing tailored pricing strategies. One potential risk is alienating certain customer segments by focusing too narrowly on a specific audience. For instance, if a business adopts a premium pricing strategy targeting high-income individuals, it may inadvertently exclude price-sensitive customers who could have been interested in its offerings had they been more affordable. This could limit the business's overall market reach and result in negative brand perception among excluded segments.

Another challenge lies in facing pricing pressure from competitors. In highly competitive markets, businesses must balance tailoring prices to attract target customers and maintain profitability. If a competitor undercuts a business's prices, it may result in a price war, which can erode profit margins and potentially damage the perceived value of the offerings. To mitigate this risk, businesses should closely monitor competitors' pricing strategies and ensure that their prices remain competitive while still reflecting the value they provide.

In summary, tailored pricing strategies can be an effective way for businesses to target specific customer segments and maximize revenue. By employing tactics such as tiered pricing plans, personalized pricing options, or bundling products and services, companies can cater to their customers' unique preferences and needs. However, businesses must consider these approaches' potential challenges and risks, such as alienating specific customer segments or facing pricing pressure from competitors. By striking the right balance and staying attuned to market dynamics, businesses can leverage tailored pricing strategies to achieve growth and success.

To further illustrate the effectiveness of tailored pricing strategies, let us examine additional examples from various industries. A prominent example can be found in the software-as-a-service (SaaS) sector. Many SaaS companies offer tiered subscription plans to cater to different customer segments based on their requirements and willingness to pay. For instance, a basic plan may provide limited features at a lower price point, while more advanced plans with additional features are offered at higher prices. This allows businesses to attract diverse customers, from small startups to large enterprises, maximizing revenue opportunities.

In the retail industry, dynamic pricing is another noteworthy pricing strategy that has gained traction. Businesses can adjust their prices to optimize sales and profitability by utilizing data analytics and real-time market demand. For example, an online retailer might offer special promotions during peak shopping or reduce prices for slow-selling products to clear inventory. This approach enables retailers to respond swiftly to changing market conditions, ensuring their pricing remains competitive and in tune with customer expectations.

The hospitality industry also offers valuable insights into successful pricing strategies. Hotels often employ revenue management techniques to optimize room rates based on seasonality, occupancy levels, and local events. By adjusting prices according to demand, hotels can maximize revenue and maintain profitability even during periods of lower occupancy.

As we conclude this chapter, let us reiterate the key takeaways: effectively tailoring prices to a business's unique value proposition, competitive landscape, and target customer segments is for success. High-volume, low-margin, and premium pricing strategies each have advantages and challenges, and businesses must carefully consider which approach aligns best with their product categories and target markets. Real-world examples from various industries demonstrate how companies have successfully implemented tailored pricing strategies, emphasizing the importance of understanding one's value proposition, competitive landscape, and target customer segments.

It is time for you to examine your business pricing strategy. Think about the fact that your business may have its unique characteristics. Ask yourself how these pricing strategies might apply to your situation, and determine if they are worth pursuing based on what has been presented here. Your unique pricing approach can differentiate you from competitors and help you attract more customers in today's highly competitive environment. If you take some time to reflect upon your business and pricing needs, you will be better equipped to develop a customized solution to help take your company to new heights.

Strategies for Increasing Profit Margins

To begin, we will explore practical tips for reducing expenses, which is one of the critical elements in driving up profit margins. Negotiating better deals with suppliers can considerably impact your bottom line. By forming strong relationships with suppliers and leveraging your purchasing power, you can secure favorable pricing and terms that directly benefit your business. This approach reduces costs and enhances the competitiveness of your offerings in the market.

Another effective strategy for cost reduction lies in implementing energy-efficient practices within your retail operations. This can encompass many initiatives, from installing energy-saving lighting and equipment to adopting intelligent building technologies that optimize heating, cooling, and ventilation systems. Such measures contribute to lower utility bills and demonstrate a commitment to environmental sustainability, which can resonate positively with today's increasingly eco-conscious consumers.

In summary, increasing profit margins in retail businesses hinges on carefully evaluating and minimizing expenses while maximizing customer value. Incorporating cost-cutting strategies such as negotiating better deals with suppliers and embracing energy-efficient practices can lay the foundation for a more prosperous and successful retail enterprise.

To illustrate the effectiveness of these cost-cutting strategies, let us examine a few real-world examples. A well-known supermarket chain implemented supplier negotiation and energy-efficient practices to reduce expenses significantly. By renegotiating contracts with suppliers, they secured lower prices for bulk purchases, resulting in substantial cost savings. Additionally, this supermarket invested in energy-efficient lighting, refrigeration systems, and temperature control measures, leading to a marked decrease in utility costs. As a result, the company's profit margins improved considerably, demonstrating that these strategies are feasible and can yield tangible results.

With a solid foundation of expense reduction in place, it becomes essential to focus on increasing average transaction value, another critical factor in enhancing profit margins.

One way to achieve this is through upselling and cross-selling techniques that encourage customers to spend more on each visit to your retail establishment.

Upselling refers to persuading customers to buy a higher-priced item or an upgraded version of the product they initially intended to purchase. This can be achieved through various methods, such as showcasing the benefits of the premium option, offering incentives like discounts or freebies, or presenting compelling product comparisons.

Conversely, cross-selling involves suggesting additional complementary products or services related to the customer's original selection. By skillfully bundling items together and highlighting their combined value, you create opportunities for customers to see the advantages of purchasing the entire package, ultimately increasing their spending.

For instance, a local electronics store may offer a discounted bundle consisting of a laptop, carrying case, and wireless mouse, providing added value to the customer while increasing the average transaction value for the business. Similarly, a clothing retailer might suggest coordinating accessories or matching garments that complement the customer's initial choice, enticing them to purchase more items and boosting their overall expenditure.

Retail businesses can significantly improve their profit margins by implementing strategic cost-cutting measures and focusing on increasing average transaction value through upselling and cross-selling techniques. These combined efforts will contribute to your enterprise's overall success and sustainability in a competitive market landscape.

Building on the concepts of upselling and cross-selling, bundling products or services is another effective strategy to increase average transaction value. Bundling involves offering a combination of complementary items at a slightly reduced price compared to purchasing each individually. This approach provides customers with value-added packages, making it more enticing for them to spend more while benefiting from perceived savings.

Consider a home improvement store that offers a bundle consisting of a drill, a set of drill bits, and a tool bag. By packaging these items together and pricing them lower than their costs, the store presents an attractive deal to customers, encouraging them to increase their spending. The perceived value of the bundled package can outweigh the desire to purchase only a single item, resulting in a higher transaction value for the retailer.

Numerous businesses have successfully implemented bundling strategies, significantly increasing their average transaction values. One notable example is a popular fast-food chain that introduced combo meals, combining a burger, fries, and a beverage at a lower price than if purchased separately. This strategy simplifies customer decision-making and encourages them to spend more on the bundled offer rather than individual items. As a result, the fast-food chain experienced a substantial boost in its average transaction value and overall revenue.

Another case study is from a high-end cosmetics brand that created gift sets containing best-selling makeup and skincare products. These sets were offered at a discounted rate compared to purchasing each item individually, attracting customers seeking luxury beauty items at a more accessible price point. Through this bundling approach, the cosmetics brand effectively increased its average transaction value and expanded its customer base by appealing to its existing clientele and those who may have otherwise considered the brand out of their budget.

By offering value-added bundles of complementary products

or services, retailers can create a win-win situation for their business and customers. Customers benefit from the perceived savings and convenience of purchasing a complete package, while retailers enjoy increased transaction values and potentially higher profit margins. Combining this strategy with the previously discussed cost-cutting measures and upselling and cross-selling techniques can contribute to overall business success in the competitive retail landscape.

Building customer loyalty is a vital aspect of any successful retail business. A loyal customer base leads to repeat business and increases the likelihood of word-of-mouth marketing, contributing significantly to long-term profitability. Companies can employ various techniques, such as personalized marketing campaigns and loyalty programs, to foster this sense of customer loyalty and commitment.

Personalized marketing campaigns are designed to make customers feel valued and understood by tailoring promotional messages, offers, and product recommendations based on their preferences, purchase history, and browsing behaviors. By leveraging data analytics and customer insights, retailers can create highly targeted campaigns that resonate with specific audience segments, leading to increased engagement, conversion rates, and customer satisfaction.

On the other hand, loyalty programs reward customers for their continued patronage by offering incentives such as discounts, points, or exclusive benefits. These programs provide tangible value to customers while encouraging them to continue shopping with the retailer, thus fostering a sense of loyalty and commitment.

A major global coffee chain known for its personalized rewards program is one shining example of a business that has successfully built customer loyalty through these strategies. This program allows customers to earn points for every purchase, which can be redeemed for complimentary beverages, food items, or merchandise. Additionally, loyalty program members receive exclusive offers and promotions tailored to their purchasing habits, further enhancing their connection to the brand. Through this powerful combination of personalization and rewards, the coffee chain boasts a fiercely loyal customer base and thrives in an increasingly competitive market.

Another example comes from a popular online retailer that excels at creating personalized customer shopping experiences. By analyzing customer data, this e-commerce giant provides individualized product recommendations, offers, and curated content, making each user feel like the website was designed specifically for them. The company's comprehensive loyalty program further strengthens the bond between the retailer and its customers by offering exclusive deals, faster shipping, and access to additional services. This personalized approach has played a significant role in the company's meteoric rise and ability to retain customers, leading to consistently high-profit margins.

Building customer loyalty is an essential component of retail success. By implementing personalized marketing campaigns and establishing effective loyalty programs, businesses can foster lasting relationships with their customers while reaping the benefits of increased retention and higher profit margins.

While building customer loyalty is essential, diversifying product lines is another pivotal aspect of retail success. Expanding the array of products or services attracts a broader customer base and creates new sales opportunities. In doing so, businesses can maximize their revenue potential while ensuring they cater to their customers' varying preferences and needs.

To successfully diversify product lines, it is to identify complementary products or services that align with existing offerings and resonate with the target market. The goal is to find items that enhance or complement the core products, offering customers a more comprehensive and satisfying shopping experience. For example, a store specializing in gourmet kitchenware may consider adding high-quality spices, oils, and condiments to its lineup to provide customers with a one-stop shop for all their culinary needs.

Businesses should begin by conducting thorough market research examining current trends and consumer demands within their industry. This process entails analyzing competitors' portfolios, identifying potential market gaps, and understanding their target audience's unique desires. By gathering this valuable information, retailers can decide which products or services to introduce.

Once a list of potential complementary items has been compiled, the next step is to evaluate the feasibility of incorporating these new products or services into the existing business model. Factors such as production costs, inventory management, and required resources must be considered. Retailers should also assess the potential profit margins of introducing new items to ensure the expansion aligns with overall business objectives.

In summary, diversifying product lines is an effective strategy for attracting a broader customer base and increasing sales opportunities. By identifying and integrating complementary products or services that align with existing offerings and appeal to the target market, retailers can optimize their revenue potential while catering to the diverse needs of their customers.

To further illustrate the effectiveness of diversifying product lines, let us examine a few case studies of businesses that have successfully expanded their offerings and achieved higher profit margins. One example is a small local bookstore that recognized its clientele's growing demand for stationery and gift items. By carefully selecting an assortment of high-quality journals, pens, and novelty gifts, the store was able to attract new customers and increase its sales revenue by 25% within just six months.

Another notable success story involves a boutique fitness studio initially focusing solely on group exercise classes. The studio introduced a line of healthy snacks and beverages upon iden-tifying an opportunity to cater to clients' nutritional needs. This strategic move boosted the average transaction value and enhanced the overall customer experience, leading to increased loyalty and word-of-mouth referrals.

In today's technology-driven business landscape, retailers can leverage cutting-edge tools and innovations to enhance profitability. One such innovation is the use of AI-powered inventory management systems. These intelligent solutions utilize machine learning algorithms to analyze historical sales data and accurately forecast future demand patterns. Consequently, retailers can optimize stock levels, reduce carrying costs, and minimize the risk of lost sales due to stock-outs or overstock situations.

Personalized marketing automation is another trend that can significantly impact a retail business's bottom line. By harnessing the power of customer data and advanced analytics, retailers can create highly targeted marketing campaigns tailored to individual preferences and behaviors. For instance, a clothing store may send personalized emails to customers who recently viewed a specific item, offering special discounts or showcasing complementary products. Such targeted efforts can lead to higher conversion rates, increased customer loyalty, and more significant profit margins.

Diversifying product lines and embracing new technologies are essential strategies for retailers seeking to thrive in today's competitive landscape. By learning from real-world examples and staying informed about emerging trends, business owners can make more informed decisions and continually refine their approach to achieve lasting success.

The potential benefits of adopting innovative technologies such as AI-powered inventory management systems and personalized marketing automation are immense. For instance, a small boutique implementing an AI-driven inventory management system saw a 15% reduction in stock obsolescence and a 10%

increase in sales due to better product availability. The intelligent algorithms enabled the store owner to make data-driven decisions about what items to stock and when, resulting in less waste and more satisfied customers.

Another example is a specialty food retailer that utilized personalized marketing automation to create targeted email campaigns for its customers. The retailer could send relevant offers and product recommendations tailored to individual tastes by analyzing past purchase data and customer preferences. This approach led to a 20% increase in open rates, a 10% rise in click-through rates, and a 5% boost in overall profit margins.

As we've seen throughout this chapter, there are several key strategies for increasing profit margins in retail. First, retailers can significantly improve their bottom line by reducing expenses by negotiating better deals with suppliers and implementing cost-saving measures like energy-efficient practices. Second, increasing average transaction value through upselling, cross-selling, and bundling products or services can encourage customers to spend more. Third, building customer loyalty through personalized marketing campaigns and loyalty programs is essential for retaining clients and ensuring repeat business. Fourth, diversifying product lines helps attract a broader customer base and increases sales opportunities. Lastly, embracing new technologies and trends, such as AI-powered inventory management systems and personalized marketing automation, can further enhance profitability and position businesses for long-term success.

In summary, the strategies discussed in this chapter have

proven effective in increasing profit margins for various retail businesses. By implementing these methods and continually assessing their impact, retailers can adapt to ever-changing market conditions and secure a prosperous future for their enterprise.

As a retailer seeking to increase profit margins and achieve sustainable success, it is that you take the insights gleaned from this chapter and apply them diligently to your own business. Embrace these strategies steadfastly and focus on continuous improvement, adapting to the ever-evolving retail landscape.

Begin by assessing your current expenses and identifying areas where cost-saving measures can be implemented. Negotiate with suppliers to secure more favorable deals and establish energy-efficient practices to reduce overhead costs. In doing so, you will be laying the foundation for improved profit margins.

Next, turn your attention to increasing average transaction values. Develop effective upselling, cross-selling, and bundling strategies that entice customers to spend more.

This will boost revenue and strengthen customer relationships by providing solutions tailored to their needs.

The importance of fostering customer loyalty cannot be over-stated. Implement personalized marketing campaigns and loyalty programs that resonate with your target audience. By nurturing long-lasting relationships with your clientele, you'll reap the benefits of increased retention rates and higher profit margins.

Diversifying your product lines is yet another powerful strategy for retailers. Identify complementary products or services that align with your existing offerings and appeal to your target market. This will expand your customer base and create additional sales opportunities.

Finally, stay informed about emerging technologies and trends within the retail industry.

Consider adopting AI-powered inventory management systems, personalized marketing automation, or other innovative solutions that can further enhance your profitability.

The key to thriving in the ever-evolving retail industry lies in implementing these proven strategies, coupled with a mindset of continuous improvement and adaptation.

By applying the lessons learned from successful businesses and embracing change, you position yourself for long-term success and sustained growth.

The Ethics of Pricing

To better understand the role pricing plays in the retail industry, it is essential to explore the psychology behind it. At the core of pricing psychology lies the customers' perception of value – assessing the worth, desirability, or usefulness of a product or service relative to its price. Various factors influence this perception, ranging from the price presentation to the emotions associated with purchasing.

One key component in shaping customers' perception of value is contrasting prices.

People are presented with multiple options and compare the different offerings to determine the best value. Retailers can capitalize on this tendency by strategically positioning their products and services alongside other items with varying price points.

This comparison can make specific options appear more attractive and encourage consumers to purchase based on perceived value.

Another aspect of pricing psychology revolves around the power of numbers. Research has shown that customers often respond favorably to prices that end in '9' or '5,' as these digits carry a psychological weight that makes them feel like they are receiving a deal. Additionally, round numbers for higher-priced items can convey a sense of quality and trustworthiness, further influencing customers' perception of value.

Emotions also play a significant role in the psychology of pricing. When customers associate positive emotions with a particular product or service, they are more likely to perceive it as valuable. Retailers can evoke such emotions through various means, including appealing visuals, compelling narratives, and even sensory experiences. By creating an emotional connection with their customers, businesses can foster a sense of loyalty that ultimately drives repeat purchases and long-term success.

Understanding pricing psychology is vital for retailers seeking to establish fair and practical pricing practices. By considering the factors influencing customers' perception of value, businesses can make informed decisions about their pricing strategies, ultimately nurturing customer trust and loyalty.

As a concept in pricing, anchoring is in shaping customers' price expectations. The anchor serves as a reference point for customers to evaluate the value of subsequent prices. For instance, a store may display an expensive luxury item next to a more affordable option, causing customers to perceive the latter as a bargain. This mental benchmark influences their purchasing decisions and encourages them to perceive the lower-priced product as desirable.

To illustrate this, imagine entering a retail store with shelves lined neatly with diverse products. In one section, you see a prominently displayed sophisticated gadget priced at $300. Your eyes then shift to another similar gadget, less extravagant yet functional, placed nearby with a price tag of $150. The initial exposure to the $300 price point is an anchor, making the $150 option seem like a much better deal.

Framing, another essential component of pricing psychology, highlights how presenting prices in different contexts can affect customers' willingness to pay. How a price is framed can significantly impact customers' perception of its value, ultimately influencing their purchase decisions.

Consider a clothing store offering a discount on a particular item. One sign displays "30% off" while another presents the same discount as "$30 off." Although both options provide the same monetary savings, customers may react differently based on the framing. A percentage discount might seem more enticing to those who perceive it as a more significant reduction, while a fixed dollar amount may appear more attractive to others who prefer a tangible saving. Retailers must carefully consider framing their discounts and promotions to capture the attention and interest of various customer segments.

The power of framing extends beyond just discounts and promotions. For example, suppose a high-quality product is offered at a premium price. In that case, emphasizing its craftsmanship, unique features, and long-term benefits can justify the cost and make customers more willing to pay. By presenting the price within the context of exceptional quality, retailers can positively influence customers' perception of value and encourage them to purchase.

The concepts of anchoring and framing are integral to understanding the dynamics of pricing in the retail industry. By using these tools effectively, businesses can shape customers' price expectations and create contexts that enhance the perceived value of their offerings. Ultimately, this will increase customer satisfaction, trust, and loyalty, laying the foundation for long-term success.

Reference pricing is another essential concept in the realm of retail pricing strategies. It refers to comparing a product's price to a standard or benchmark price to create an impression of value. For instance, a customer might perceive a $100 item as expensive in isolation but may deem it a good deal if they see its competitor's products are priced at $150. By providing this point of reference, retailers can influence customers' perception of value and encourage them to purchase.

To capitalize on reference pricing, businesses should present their products alongside comparable alternatives while emphasizing the benefits and features distinguishing their offerings from competitors. This approach will demonstrate the relative value of their products and showcase their unique selling points, fostering a sense of exclusivity and desirability that can further motivate customers to buy.

In addition to leveraging reference pricing, businesses should strive to make their pricing more transparent and comprehensible to customers. One effective strategy is to provide itemized pricing, which breaks down the cost of individual components or services included in a product or package. This method allows customers to understand precisely what they are paying for and appreciate the value they receive from each element.

For example, a furniture retailer could display the cost of materials, craftsmanship, and shipping separately, helping customers appreciate the quality and effort invested in creating their desired piece. Similarly, a service provider like a wedding planner could itemize the various aspects of their offering, such as venue booking, catering, and decoration, enabling clients to grasp the value of each component and make informed decisions.

Another aspect of transparent pricing is avoiding hidden fees. Customers will likely feel frustrated and deceived if they discover unexpected costs during the purchasing process, undermining trust and loyalty. Hence, retailers must ensure that all applicable taxes, shipping fees, and other charges are communicated upfront, leaving no room for confusion or disappointment.

By implementing these strategies, retailers can create value for their customers while fostering trust and transparency. Ultimately, these practices will enhance customer satisfaction, loyalty, and long-term success in the highly competitive retail landscape.

Clear pricing communication is vital to ethical pricing practices in the retail industry.

Retailers must provide detailed product information and pricing options to communicate prices effectively. This includes presenting customers with accurate descriptions of the product's features, benefits, and any potential limitations. By doing so, customers can make informed decisions based on a comprehensive understanding of the value they will receive from their purchase.

One effective way to communicate pricing options is to present tiered price structures catering to different customer preferences and budgets. For example, a software company could offer various subscription plans with distinct feature sets and pricing tiers, allowing customers to select the option that best suits their needs and financial constraints. This approach empowers customers by granting them control over purchasing decisions while demonstrating the retailer's commitment to accommodating diverse consumer requirements.

Simplifying complex pricing structures is another essential component of clear pricing communication. Retailers should streamline their pricing models, ensuring customers can easily understand and compare prices between products or service offerings. This may involve consolidating multiple fees into a single, all-inclusive price or providing precise visual representations of pricing breakdowns using charts or infographics.

To guide businesses in simplifying their pricing structures, consider the following steps:

1. Evaluate the existing pricing model: Begin by assessing the current pricing structure to identify areas of complexity or confusion for customers. This may include hidden fees, overly complicated discounts, or unclear terms and conditions.

2. Eliminate unnecessary components: Remove redundant or non-essential elements from the pricing structure that do not contribute to the product's value or customer experience. This may involve combining similar charges or fees into a single cost or discarding outdated promotions.

3. Organize pricing information: Arrange pricing details logically and easily digestible. This may include grouping related charges, consistently displaying prices, or using visually appealing graphics to illustrate price comparisons.

4. Test and refine: Seek customer feedback on the revised pricing structure to ensure it is easily understood and meets their needs. Based on feedback, adjust the model as necessary and continuously monitor its effectiveness.

By prioritizing clear pricing communication and simplifying complex pricing structures, retailers can create a more transparent and positive customer shopping experience.

This approach will foster trust and loyalty and empower consumers to make informed decisions that align with their unique needs, preferences, and budget constraints. In turn, these practices will contribute to businesses' long-term success and sustainability in the ever-evolving retail industry.

One notable example of a business successfully implementing ethical pricing practices is Everlane, an online clothing retailer. Known for its commitment to price transparency, Everlane shares the exact costs associated with each product's production, including materials, labor, shipping, and even taxes. By providing this level of detail, customers gain insight into the actual value of the products they purchase and can better understand the rationale behind their prices.

Another instance of transparent pricing policies comes from Buffer, a social media management platform. Buffer's pricing model is straightforward, with tiered subscription plans that cater to different user needs and budgets. Each plan is clearly outlined on its website, allowing potential customers to quickly compare features and make informed decisions. Additionally, Buffer offers a detailed breakdown of how subscription fees support various aspects of the platform's operations, fostering greater trust and understanding between the company and its users.

Ethical pricing practices, such as those employed by Everlane and Buffer, significantly impact customer trust and loyalty. When businesses prioritize transparency and fairness in their pricing structures, they demonstrate respect for their customers' intelligence and empower them to make purchasing decisions based on accurate information. This approach fosters a sense of trust and confidence in the brand, encouraging customers to continue patronizing the business and recommend it to others.

Moreover, these practices contribute to long-term business benefits by cultivating strong customer relationships. As consumers become increasingly savvy and discerning, they are more likely to gravitate toward companies that demonstrate ethical behavior and prioritize customer satisfaction. In turn, these businesses enjoy increased customer retention rates, more favorable word-of-mouth marketing, and, ultimately, more significant revenue growth.

Implementing ethical pricing practices is not only a matter of fairness and integrity but also a strategic move that can enhance a business's reputation, strengthen customer relationships, and drive long-term success. By showcasing real-world examples like Everlane and Buffer, retailers can draw inspiration and motivation to develop their transparent pricing policies and join the ranks of businesses prioritizing customer trust and loyalty.

Case Study 1: Patagonia

Known for its eco-conscious outdoor gear and clothing, Patagonia has built strong customer relationships by adhering to ethical pricing practices. The company's "Ironclad Guarantee" ensures that customers can return items for repair, replacement, or refund if they are unsatisfied with the performance or quality. This guarantee reinforces the brand's commitment to providing long-lasting products at a fair price and engenders customer trust and loyalty.

Moreover, Patagonia communicates its dedication to sustainability and environmental responsibility through its pricing strategy. By offering fair wages to factory workers and using environmentally friendly materials, the company justifies higher price points for its products while simultaneously appealing to customers' values and sense of social responsibility.

Case Study 2: Warby Parker

Warby Parker, a famous eyewear retailer, has distinguished itself from competitors by offering high-quality glasses at affordable prices. Through a direct-to-consumer model and transparent pricing structure, the company eliminates traditional markup and passes the savings on to customers.

Warby Parker emphasizes the importance of providing excellent service and value to build strong customer relationships. For example, their "Home Try-On" program allows customers to test out frames in the comfort of their homes before purchasing, making the decision-making process more convenient and enjoyable. By focusing on customer satisfaction and maintaining an ethical pricing strategy, Warby Parker has established a loyal customer base that appreciates the fairness and clarity of their pricing.

Retailers should recognize the importance of implementing ethical pricing practices in their businesses. Case studies like Patagonia and Warby Parker demonstrate that prioritizing transparency, fairness, and customer satisfaction can lead to strong customer relationships and long-term success. By providing clear communication, avoiding hidden fees, and simplifying complex pricing structures, businesses can foster customer trust and loyalty, ultimately leading to greater revenue growth.

Considering how your retail business can benefit from ethical pricing practices, consider the lessons learned from these thriving companies. Remember that offering fair prices and being transparent about your costs is a matter of integrity and a factor in building lasting relationships with your customers. Your commitment to ethical pricing will set you apart from competitors and help you thrive in today's competitive marketplace.

Marketing and Pricing

U nderstanding the target market is essential when tailoring marketing efforts to communicate the value proposition of a product or service. By identifying the specific needs, preferences, and expectations of the intended audience, businesses are better equipped to develop marketing messages that resonate with potential customers. This not only increases the likelihood of attracting and retaining customers but also ensures that marketing resources are allocated efficiently to maximize return on investment.

In order to create marketing campaigns that effectively convey the value of a product or service to the target market, businesses must first have a comprehensive understanding of their customer base. This involves analyzing demographic data, such as age, gender, income, and geographic location, as well as psychographic information, including interests, values, and lifestyle choices. With this knowledge in hand, businesses can craft messages that speak directly to the pain points, desires, and aspirations of their target audience, thereby increasing the perceived value of their offerings and supporting their pricing strategy.

Ultimately, the success of any marketing campaign hinges on its ability to demonstrate the value of a product or service to the target market. By taking the time to understand the unique characteristics and preferences of the intended audience, businesses can develop tailored marketing messages that convey the benefits and uniqueness of their products or services, thereby justifying price points and driving sales.

Market research and customer segmentation play a role in identifying the most effective marketing channels for reaching the target audience. A thorough analysis of the target market, including their preferences and behaviors, is essential to determine the best means of communication that will resonate with them. This information allows businesses to invest resources into marketing channels that are most likely to yield positive results, ensuring a higher return on investment.

Various marketing channels can be utilized to deliver value to customers, each with its own strengths and limitations. Print advertising, for example, offers a tangible medium that can captivate audiences through engaging visuals and creative design. However, its reach may be limited by circulation numbers and geographical constraints. Television advertising, on the other hand, provides an opportunity for businesses to showcase their products and services through dynamic visuals and sound, but may come with a higher cost to produce and air advertisements.

Radio advertising offers the advantage of reaching a wide audience at a relatively low cost; however, it relies solely on audio input, which may not be as captivating as visual channels. Social media marketing allows businesses to engage directly with their target audience and create personalized content tailored to their interests, while also benefiting from the potential virality of shareable content. The limitation of social media marketing lies in the constantly changing algorithms that may affect visibility and reach.

Email marketing is an effective channel for businesses looking to maintain direct communication with their customers, offering targeted promotions and updates.

However, the effectiveness of email marketing hinges on recipients opening and engaging with the messages, which may be hindered by an inundated inbox or ineffective subject lines. Content marketing, encompassing blog posts, articles, videos, and other forms of informative material, can help establish a business as an authority in their industry and build trust with customers. The challenge with content marketing lies in creating consistent, high-quality content that stands out among competitors and generates interest from the target audience.

Identifying the right mix of marketing channels is a component of developing a successful marketing strategy that supports the pricing model. By conducting in-depth market research and thoroughly understanding customer preferences, businesses can make informed decisions about which channels to invest in for maximum impact. By leveraging the strengths of each channel while being mindful of their limitations, businesses can effectively communicate their value proposition, support their pricing strategy, and ultimately drive sales.

To effectively support a business's pricing strategy, one must consider a variety of marketing tactics that can emphasize the value and benefits of products or services.

Some of these tactics include value-based pricing, bundling, upselling, and offering discounts and promotions.

Value-based pricing is a method in which prices are set according to the perceived value of a product or service to the customer, rather than based solely on production costs or competitors' prices. This approach allows businesses to justify higher price points, provided they can demonstrate the unique value proposition offered to their customers. For example, Apple Inc. has successfully implemented value-based pricing for its line of iPhones, iPads, and Mac computers. By focusing on the superior design, user experience, and innovative features of their products, Apple justifies premium pricing that sets them apart from other technology companies.

Bundling is another marketing tactic that can support a business's pricing strategy. By combining multiple products or services into a single package, businesses can offer customers a perceived discount, driving sales and increasing overall revenue.

For instance, telecommunications companies often bundle services like internet, phone, and television to attract customers with the convenience and savings of a single bill.

Bundling creates a sense of value for customers, as they perceive that they are getting more for their money.

Upselling is a technique used to encourage customers to purchase a higher-priced item or add-on, often by emphasizing the additional features or benefits of the more expensive option. For example, a car salesperson might suggest upgrading to a model with leather seats, advanced safety features, or a larger engine for an improved driving experience. Upselling not only increases the average transaction value but also enhances customer satisfaction when they perceive the added value of the higher-priced option.

Discounts and promotions are common marketing tactics employed to create a sense of urgency and incentivize customers to make a purchase. By offering limited-time deals or exclusive offers, businesses can drive sales, attract new customers, and increase brand awareness. However, overusing discounts and promotions can lead to a decrease in perceived value and damage the business's pricing strategy in the long run.

Understanding the various marketing tactics available and selecting the most appropriate ones for a specific business can greatly support a company's pricing strategy. By leveraging value-based pricing, bundling, upselling, and offering discounts and promotions, businesses can effectively communicate their unique value proposition, justify price points, and ultimately drive sales and profitability.

Crafting compelling marketing messages is an element in communicating the value of products or services being offered. Clear and concise messaging that resonates with the target audience is essential in capturing their interest and persuading them to make a purchase. A well-crafted message should convey the unique value proposition of a product or service, highlighting its features, benefits, and how it solves a problem or fulfills a need for the customer.

One powerful way to create emotional connections with customers and enhance the effectiveness of marketing messages is through storytelling. Storytelling in marketing involves weaving relatable narratives around a product or service, often focusing on the experiences and emotions associated with using it. By tapping into the power of stories, businesses can evoke feelings, foster empathy, and build trust with their audience, ultimately supporting their pricing strategies and creating a perception of value.

For instance, consider a luxury watch brand that tells the story of its heritage and craftsmanship through its marketing messages. The brand might share the history of its founders, their passion for watchmaking, and the meticulous attention to detail that goes into each timepiece. This narrative not only showcases the watch's premium quality but also evokes a sense of prestige, exclusivity, and timelessness, justifying the higher price point associated with the product.

Another example comes from the world of technology, where a company specializing in noise-canceling headphones might craft a marketing story centered around the idea of creating a personal sanctuary amid the chaos of daily life. By emphasizing the experience of escaping into one's own world, free from distractions, the company can show potential customers the value of investing in high-quality headphones that deliver superior sound and noise cancellation.

It's important to note that while storytelling is an effective marketing tool, it must be authentic and relevant to truly resonate with the target audience. To achieve this, businesses should focus on understanding their customers' needs, desires, and pain points, using this insight to create stories that genuinely connect with their experiences.

Crafting compelling marketing messages is essential for effectively communicating the value of products or services and supporting a business's pricing strategy. By leveraging the power of storytelling, businesses can create emotional connections with customers and reinforce the perceived value of their offerings, ultimately driving sales and profitability. In the next chapter, we will explore additional strategies for enhancing customer perceptions of price through testimonials and aligning marketing efforts with pricing strategies.

In the world of marketing, customer testimonials and reviews play a role in shaping perceptions of price. These firsthand accounts from satisfied customers serve as powerful endorsements that can greatly influence potential buyers. In fact, research has shown that 92% of consumers trust recommendations from people they know, and 70% of consumers trust online reviews from other customers (Nielsen, 2015).

One strategy for leveraging positive customer feedback to reinforce the value of products or services is to showcase testimonials prominently on a business's website, in marketing materials, or even within the product packaging. By doing so, businesses can provide social proof that their offerings are worth the investment, ultimately influencing purchasing decisions and supporting pricing strategies.

Another approach involves turning customer success stories into case studies that demonstrate real-world benefits and positive outcomes. These detailed narratives not only highlight the value of a product or service but also inspire confidence in potential customers by showcasing how others have found success using the offering.

Moving forward, it is essential for businesses to align marketing efforts with pricing strategies. This alignment enables companies to create perceived value and differentiate themselves from competitors. For instance, if a business's pricing strategy is based on offering premium products at a higher price point, its marketing efforts should focus on communicating the unique features and superior quality that justify this price.

Conversely, if a company chooses a competitive pricing strategy, emphasizing affordability and value for money, marketing efforts should be directed towards showcasing cost-saving benefits and attractive promotions. No matter the chosen pricing strategy, the key is to ensure that all marketing activities consistently support and reinforce the underlying pricing objectives.

In summary, understanding the power of customer testimonials and reviews, and effectively aligning marketing efforts with pricing strategies are vital components of successful marketing campaigns. By doing so, businesses can enhance customer perceptions of price, create perceived value, and set themselves apart from their competitors. With these principles in mind, businesses can develop well-rounded, focused marketing campaigns that support their pricing strategies and drive long-term success.

To further illustrate the effectiveness of marketing campaigns that support a business's pricing strategy, let us examine some real-world examples. One such example is Apple Inc., a company known for its premium-priced products and strong emphasis on innovation and design. Apple's marketing efforts consistently focus on highlighting the unique features and superior quality of their products, justifying the higher price point.

By targeting an audience that values cutting-edge technology and aesthetics, Apple has managed to create a customer base that is loyal and willing to pay a premium for their offerings.

Another example is Costco Wholesale Corporation, which employs a different pricing strategy by offering competitively priced products in bulk quantities. Costco's marketing efforts emphasize the cost-saving benefits of membership and the wide variety of products available under one roof. By targeting value-conscious consumers who prioritize affordability and convenience, Costco has successfully attracted a dedicated customer base, resulting in increased profitability.

These examples demonstrate how tailored marketing tactics can effectively communicate the value proposition of a product or service, supporting the chosen pricing strategy and ultimately contributing to a business's success.

However, it is essential to remember that marketing strategies should not remain static.

To ensure continued alignment with pricing objectives, businesses must regularly evaluate and adjust their marketing efforts. This ongoing process involves tracking key performance indicators (KPIs), such as customer acquisition cost, conversion rates, and return on investment, to determine the efficacy of various marketing channels and tactics.

By monitoring KPIs and analyzing data, businesses can make informed decisions about where to allocate marketing resources and how to refine their messaging to better target their desired audience. For example, if data reveals that a particular marketing channel has low conversion rates, it may be prudent to explore alternative channels or adjust the messaging to better resonate with the target audience.

Successful marketing campaigns require a keen understanding of target audiences, strategic alignment with pricing objectives, and ongoing evaluation and adjustment based on data-driven insights. By implementing these principles, businesses can create impactful marketing strategies that not only support their pricing decisions but also contribute to long-term profitability and growth.

In summary, the key points discussed in this chapter underscore the role marketing plays in setting and promoting prices. The effectiveness of any pricing strategy is contingent upon a well-executed marketing plan that targets the right audience, communicates the value proposition clearly, and remains adaptable to changes in customer preferences and market conditions.

The first step towards achieving this goal is understanding the target market and tailoring marketing efforts to effectively communicate the unique value offered by the products or services. This includes conducting market research and segmenting customers based on various factors such as demographics, interests, and purchase behavior.

We also examined different marketing channels – from print advertising and television to social media and content marketing – and evaluated their strengths and limitations.

These channels can be used in tandem to deliver value to customers, provided they align with the business's pricing objectives and resonate with the target audience.

Various marketing tactics, including value-based pricing, bundling, upselling, and offering discounts and promotions, can further support a business's pricing strategy.

When coupled with powerful storytelling techniques and positive customer testimonials, these tactics can create emotional connections with customers and shape their perceptions of price and value.

As a business owner or marketer, it is important to frequently evaluate and adjust marketing strategies in response to data-driven insights. By tracking key performance indicators (KPIs) and making informed decisions, businesses can optimize their marketing efforts and ensure alignment with their pricing strategies.

Now is the time to apply these concepts and strategies to your own business. Reflect on your current marketing efforts and ask yourself whether they are effectively supporting your pricing objectives. Are you reaching the right target audience? Are your marketing messages clear and compelling? Are you leveraging the most appropriate marketing channels and tactics?

To further enhance your marketing skills, we encourage you to explore additional resources and continue learning about effective marketing tactics that can support your pricing strategies. Seek out case studies, attend webinars, read industry publications, and network with fellow professionals to stay informed of the latest trends and best practices in marketing.

Remember, a well-crafted marketing plan is instrumental in setting and promoting prices that not only cover costs and generate profits but also reflect the true value of your products or services. By harnessing the power of marketing, you can create strong customer relationships, differentiate your business from competitors, and pave the way for long-term success.

As we move forward, it is to recognize that pricing and marketing strategies are not the only factors determining a business's success. In the next chapter, we will explore another essential element of running a thriving venture: effective sales techniques.

These techniques play a critical role in converting your target audience's interest into actual sales, ensuring that your marketing efforts translate into measurable results.

The upcoming chapter will delve into various sales methodologies, negotiation tactics, and relationship-building skills that can significantly impact a business's bottom line.

Just as you have learned to align your marketing strategy with your pricing goals, you will discover the importance of synchronizing your sales approach with these objectives, ultimately maximizing revenue potential and customer satisfaction.

By incorporating the concepts from this current chapter on marketing and pricing strategies with the forthcoming insights on effective sales techniques, you will be well-equipped with a comprehensive understanding of how to optimize your business's performance. The integration of these key components will undoubtedly lead to a more robust and successful enterprise.

So, prepare to expand your knowledge even further as we continue our journey towards mastering the art of conducting business effectively. Stay tuned for an in-depth exploration of sales techniques that will complement and enhance your existing marketing and pricing strategies, propelling your business to new heights.

Pricing in the Digital Age

The digital landscape has created a paradigm shift in how retail businesses approach pricing strategies. With e-commerce gaining immense traction, traditional brick-and-mortar establishments face new challenges when establishing competitive prices that attract customers while maintaining profitability.

Online retail has emerged as a dominant force in the industry, prompting businesses to reassess their pricing frameworks and adapt to this evolving market. The exponential growth of e-commerce platforms has led to increased competition, with consumers having easy access to many choices at their fingertips. This, in turn, has made price comparison effortless for shoppers, placing additional pressure on retailers to create effective pricing models.

In response to these challenges, big data and artificial intelligence (AI) play roles in revolutionizing pricing in the digital age. These cutting-edge technologies enable businesses to analyze vast amounts of information and extract valuable insights that can be leveraged to optimize pricing decisions.

Big data refers to the massive volume of structured and unstructured data generated by various sources such as social media, customer transactions, and web browsing patterns.

By harnessing the power of big data, retailers can gain a deeper understanding of customer preferences, habits, and behaviors. This wealth of information allows them to identify trends, monitor competitor pricing, and forecast demand, supporting informed decision-making on product offerings and pricing structures.

Artificial intelligence complements extensive data analysis by employing advanced algorithms and machine learning techniques to process and interpret complex datasets.

AI-powered pricing tools can dynamically adjust prices based on real-time market conditions, enabling businesses to stay ahead of the competition while maximizing profit margins. Additionally, these sophisticated systems can predict future price fluctuations and facilitate strategic planning, ensuring companies remain agile and responsive to changing consumer needs and expectations.

The increasing prevalence of online retail presents both opportunities and challenges for businesses aiming to establish effective pricing strategies. By integrating big data and artificial intelligence, companies can optimize pricing decisions, enhance profitability, and maintain a competitive edge in the ever-evolving digital landscape.

Several businesses have successfully harnessed the power of

big data and artificial intelligence to optimize their pricing strategies, leading to positive outcomes in increased revenue and customer satisfaction. For instance, Amazon's dynamic pricing strategy relies heavily on massive data analysis and machine learning algorithms to adjust prices continuously based on demand, competition, and other factors. This highly responsive approach has allowed the e-commerce giant to maintain its competitive edge and attract a wide range of customers.

Similarly, airlines such as Delta and United have employed AI-driven revenue management systems to set optimal ticket prices by analyzing vast amounts of data, including historical sales, weather forecasts, competitor fares, and customer preferences. This sophisticated pricing method has enabled these airlines to maximize profits while ensuring that seats are filled, and customers receive a fair price.

As we explore the role of social media in shaping perceptions of price, it becomes clear that customer reviews and online platforms have significantly empowered customers to share their opinions and experiences. Websites like Yelp, TripAdvisor, and Google Reviews offer users the opportunity to rate and review businesses from various industries, providing a platform for consumers to voice their thoughts and engage with others who have had similar encounters.

These digital forums hold considerable sway over public opinion, as potential customers often rely on these reviews when purchasing. Moreover, they can influence a business's reputation, emphasizing the importance of maintaining a positive presence on these platforms. A single negative review might not severely impact a company, but a pattern of dissatisfaction could deter potential customers and lead to lost revenue.

In this context, it is essential for businesses to actively monitor their online reputation and engage with customers on social media platforms. Companies can demonstrate their commitment to customer satisfaction and build trust within their target market by addressing concerns, offering solutions, and showcasing positive testimonials. This proactive approach to managing online perception allows businesses to address shortcomings and leverage positive feedback to enhance their pricing strategies further.

In summary, integrating big data and artificial intelligence has revolutionized pricing strategies for various businesses, leading to increased profitability and customer satisfaction. Additionally, social media platforms and customer reviews have become key players in shaping price perceptions, necessitating companies to actively engage with their online audience and use this feedback to inform their pricing decisions.

A prime example of a business that has effectively managed its online reputation and utilized customer feedback to inform pricing decisions is the well-established e-commerce giant Amazon. Through their sophisticated review system, Amazon encourages customers to share detailed accounts of their experiences with products, which in turn fosters trust among potential buyers. By analyzing these reviews and incorporating them into their pricing algorithms, Amazon can make informed adjustments to individual product prices and the overall pricing strategy for their platform.

The company's approach to managing online reputation involves actively monitoring customer reviews, swiftly responding to queries or concerns, and addressing negative feedback head-on. This proactive approach helps maintain a positive online presence and enables Amazon to identify trends in customer satisfaction and dissatisfaction, ultimately allowing them to optimize their pricing strategy.

Another noteworthy example is the popular ride-hailing service Uber. By collecting real-time data on user ratings, feedback, and demand patterns, Uber adjusts its pricing dynamically to ensure maximum profitability while maintaining customer satisfaction.

Their surge pricing model, for instance, is based on the delicate balance between supply and demand, considering factors such as driver availability and customer willingness to pay higher rates during peak hours.

Companies must monitor and respond to customer reviews actively to emulate the success of businesses like Amazon and Uber. Practical guidance for achieving this includes:

1. Assigning a dedicated team or individual to manage the company's online reputation. This individual or team should be responsible for regularly checking customer reviews, identifying patterns or recurring issues, and engaging with customers when necessary.

2. Developing a standardized response protocol for addressing negative reviews. This protocol should include empathizing with the customer's concerns, acknowledging shortcomings, and offering appropriate solutions or compensation.

3. Encouraging satisfied customers to leave positive reviews through incentives or rewards programs. Such initiatives can counterbalance the impact of negative reviews and create a more balanced online presence.

4. Regularly analyzing customer feedback data to identify trends and areas for improvement. This information can then inform pricing decisions or other aspects of the business.

Businesses need to recognize the importance of actively monitoring and responding to customer reviews, as they play a role in shaping their online reputation and informing pricing strategies. By following practical guidance and learning from the success stories of companies such as Amazon and Uber, businesses can maintain a positive online presence while optimizing their pricing strategies for maximum profitability and customer satisfaction.

In today's digital landscape, social media platforms have emerged as powerful tools for businesses to engage with customers and build trust. These platforms play a role in pricing strategies, allowing businesses to communicate their value proposition effectively. By leveraging social media, companies can create a strong online presence that showcases their products and services while fostering a sense of trust among consumers.

One prime example of a business that has successfully employed social media to enhance its pricing strategy is the popular ride-sharing service Uber. The company has been able to use Twitter and Facebook to manage surge pricing during periods of high demand, communicating the rationale behind such pricing adjustments to their users. By being transparent about price changes, Uber has fostered greater trust among its customer base and minimized potential backlash.

Another notable case study involves the clothing retailer Everlane. This company has built its reputation on price transparency, detailing the cost breakdown of each product on its website and across social media platforms. By sharing this information openly, Everlane has established itself as an ethical brand that values fair pricing and responsible manufacturing practices. This approach resonated with consumers, increasing customer loyalty and sales.

To leverage social media effectively in shaping pricing strategies, businesses should consider the following tactics:

1. Create engaging content: Businesses must develop informative and visually appealing content communicating their value proposition to customers. This can include infographics, videos, or images that showcase a product's or service's benefits and justify its price.

2. Be transparent: Sharing the rationale behind pricing decisions can help build customer trust and foster a sense of fairness. Companies can use social media to explain factors influencing their pricing, such as production costs, market conditions, or competitor pricing.

3. Respond to customer inquiries: Engaging with customers through social media channels can help businesses address concerns, clarify misconceptions, and provide valuable insights into consumer preferences. This feedback can then refine pricing strategies and ensure they remain competitive.

4. Monitor competitor activity: Keeping a close eye on competitors' pricing strategies can help businesses identify opportunities for differentiation and adjust their pricing accordingly. Social media platforms offer valuable insights into competitor activities and market trends, making it easier for companies to stay informed and agile.

By utilizing these tactics, businesses can harness the power of social media platforms to enhance their pricing strategies and foster trust among customers. As seen in the case studies of Uber and Everlane, transparency and engagement are key factors in generating customer loyalty and driving sales in today's digital marketplace.

Managing an online reputation is for businesses in the digital age, especially in the context of pricing. If left unaddressed, negative feedback can undermine a business's credibility and deter potential customers. Therefore, companies must promptly address negative feedback, resolve customer issues, and maintain transparency in their pricing strategies.

One way to manage online reputation is by actively monitoring customer reviews on various platforms such as Google, Yelp, and social media. This allows businesses to identify trends in feedback and take necessary actions to address concerns. For instance, if multiple customers complain about an overpriced product, the company may need to reassess its pricing strategy or provide additional justification for the price point.

Businesses need to respond to negative reviews professionally and empathetically, demonstrating their commitment to customer satisfaction. Offering solutions, refunds, or discounts can help resolve customer issues and turn a negative experience into a positive one. Moreover, this proactive approach can also increase trust and loyalty among customers, who appreciate a company's willingness to admit mistakes and make amends.

Transparency is key when addressing customer concerns related to pricing. By openly discussing the factors contributing to a product's price, businesses can communicate the value they offer and justify their pricing decisions. This can be achieved through blog posts, informative videos, or social media updates, which explain the costs involved in production, distribution, and other relevant aspects.

Customer reviews play a significant role in shaping perceptions of price, as they offer insights into the experiences and opinions of real users. Positive reviews can reinforce a company's image as providing good value for money, while negative reviews can tarnish this perception. To encourage positive reviews, businesses can:

1. Request feedback: Businesses can send follow-up emails or messages asking customers to share their experiences on review platforms after a purchase or interaction. This helps gather valuable feedback and increases the likelihood of receiving positive reviews.

2. Offer incentives: Incentivizing customers to leave reviews, such as offering discounts or rewards for their next purchase, can motivate them to share their experiences online.

3. Provide exceptional service: Ultimately, the best way to encourage positive reviews is by ensuring that customers have a great experience with a product or service. This includes offering high-quality products, excellent customer service, and prompt resolution of any issues.

Businesses should remain professional and constructive when addressing negative reviews, focusing on understanding the customer's concerns and finding a solution.

Apologizing for any inconvenience caused and outlining steps taken to resolve the issue can help rebuild trust with the customer and demonstrate the company's commitment to continuous improvement.

Managing online reputation in the context of pricing requires businesses to proactively address negative feedback, resolve customer issues, and maintain transparency in their pricing strategies. By doing so, companies can effectively influence customer perceptions, build trust, and ensure long-term success in the digital age.

Maintaining a consistent and positive online presence is

paramount in today's digital age. A strong online presence establishes credibility and fosters trust among customers.

Social media platforms, such as Facebook, Twitter, Instagram, and LinkedIn, serve as invaluable tools for businesses to showcase their value proposition and connect with their target audience.

To effectively leverage social media in building trust and showcasing value, businesses should:

1. Share engaging content: Posting informative and relevant content that resonates with the target audience will help to position the business as an industry expert. This could include blog posts, articles, infographics, or short videos that provide valuable insights into the company's offerings and industry trends.

2. Be responsive: Promptly responding to customer queries and feedback on social media demonstrates that a business values its customers' opinions. Engaging in open communication and promptly addressing concerns helps build trust and foster positive customer relationships.

3. Maintain brand consistency: Ensuring that branding elements, such as colors, logos, and messaging, are consistent across all social media platforms creates a unified and recognizable brand identity. A cohesive digital presence reinforces brand recognition, which can increase customer trust and loyalty.

4. Monitor sentiment: Utilizing social listening tools to keep track of customer conversations and sentiment around a brand enables businesses to gauge public perception and identify areas where improvements may be needed. By staying attuned to customer feedback, companies can adapt their strategies and messaging to maintain a positive reputation.

As the chapter comes to a close, it is essential to emphasize the need for businesses to adapt their pricing strategies to the ever-evolving digital landscape. The increasing prevalence of e-commerce and the rise of big data and artificial intelligence have transformed how businesses approach pricing, making it for companies to stay ahead of the curve.

Readers are encouraged to harness the power of technology and online platforms to optimize their pricing decisions. By leveraging big data, artificial intelligence, and social media platforms, businesses can make informed pricing decisions that maximize profitability while fostering customer trust and loyalty.

The digital age presents challenges and opportunities for businesses to refine their pricing strategies, enhance their online reputation, and maintain strong customer relationships. Companies can thrive in today's competitive marketplace by embracing these new technologies and adapting their pricing approaches.

Adapting to Economic Fluctuations

I n the ever-changing retail industry landscape, businesses must adapt to economic fluctuations to maintain profitability. Economic shifts can impact consumer behavior, supply chain dynamics, and overall market conditions. Retailers must be agile and responsive, adjusting their strategies to remain competitive and profitable during prosperity and adversity.

One exemplary case study of a business that successfully navigated an economic downturn is that of a well-known home improvement retailer. During the financial crisis 2008, this retailer faced significant challenges, including decreased consumer spending, increased competition, and rising costs. However, through insightful decision-making and strategic planning, the company overcame these hurdles and emerged even more vital.

To combat the effects of the economic downturn, the retailer focused on three key areas:

1. Adjusting Prices

2. Managing Inventory Levels
3. Controlling Costs

Recognizing that consumers were more price-sensitive during this time, the company conducted extensive market research to identify the optimal pricing strategy. By offering competitive prices, the retailer could attract budget-conscious customers while maintaining healthy profit margins.

Inventory management was another component of the company's strategy. The retailer implemented sophisticated demand forecasting models and adopted just-in-time inventory systems to minimize stock-holding costs and reduce the risk of carrying excess or obsolete stock. At the same time, the company worked closely with suppliers to secure favorable pricing and ensure a reliable flow of goods during periods of inflation.

Lastly, the retailer placed a strong emphasis on cost control. This involved closely monitoring expenses and analyzing data to identify areas where cost reductions could be made without compromising product quality or customer experience. Examples of cost-saving measures included renegotiating supplier contracts, optimizing energy usage, streamlining operations, and implementing technology solutions to reduce labor costs.

Through these strategic initiatives, the home improvement retailer survived the economic downturn and positioned itself for future growth and success. This case study is a powerful example for other retailers of the importance of adapting to economic fluctuations and the value of implementing well-thought-out strategies in challenging market conditions.

Adjusting prices is a critical strategy for navigating economic fluctuations. During a downturn, businesses may consider lowering prices to attract customers and maintain sales volume. This approach can be efficient in retail, where consumers often seek the best deals. By offering competitive prices, retailers can appeal to budget-conscious customers while maintaining healthy profit margins.

To implement this pricing strategy effectively, retailers must conduct thorough market research to understand customer price sensitivity and competitor pricing strategies. The following step-by-step guide outlines the key aspects of conducting such research:

1. Define your research objectives: Begin by clearly articulating your market research goals. For example, you may want to understand how sensitive your customers are to price changes or how your competitors are pricing their products.

2. Identify your target audience: Determine the specific customer segments you want to research. Consider demographics, location, and purchasing behavior when defining your target audience.

3. Collect primary data: Conduct surveys, interviews, or focus groups with your target audience to gather firsthand information about their price sensitivity, preferences, and perceptions of your competitors' pricing strategies.

4. Analyze secondary data: Review existing research, industry reports, and competitor pricing information to gain further insights into customer price sensitivity and competitive pricing strategies.

5. Observe market trends: Monitor changes in market conditions, such as fluctuations in consumer spending, to identify any emerging trends that may impact your pricing decisions.

6. Conduct a competitive analysis: Assess your competitors' pricing strategies by comparing their product offerings, promotional activities, and overall pricing structures. This will help you understand how your pricing strategy compares and identify potential opportunities for differentiation.

7. Analyze your findings: Synthesize the data and insights gathered from your research to conclude customer price sensitivity and competitor pricing strategies. Use these findings to inform your own pricing decisions.

8. Test your pricing strategy: Before implementing any changes to your pricing, it is advisable to conduct small-scale tests to gauge customer reactions and measure the impact on sales volume and profitability.

9. Monitor and adjust: Continuously monitor the performance of your pricing strategy, making adjustments as needed based on market conditions and customer feedback.

By following this step-by-step guide, retailers can gain a deeper understanding of customer price sensitivity and competitor pricing strategies, enabling them to make informed decisions about adjusting prices during economic fluctuations. By doing so, they can better position themselves for success in challenging and prosperous market environments.

To further illustrate the importance of adjusting prices during economic fluctuations, let us examine the case study of a well-known electronics retailer that successfully navigated a period of inflation. During this challenging time, the company recognized the need to offset rising costs and maintain profitability by effectively adjusting their prices.

The electronics retailer began by closely monitoring market conditions and analyzing customer price sensitivity, which enabled them to make informed decisions about their pricing strategy. They found that customers were willing to pay slightly higher prices for products with advanced features or superior quality, while more price-sensitive customers gravitated towards budget-friendly options. Armed with this knowledge, the company strategically adjusted prices based on product offerings and customer preferences, ensuring they maintained a competitive edge without sacrificing profit margins.

As the company navigated through the period of inflation, it also understood the critical importance of managing inventory levels during economic fluctuations. Holding excess stock during a downturn can lead to increased carrying costs, obsolescence, and potential markdowns, negatively impacting profitability. On the other hand, securing supply during periods of inflation is to avoid stockouts and production disruptions, which could result in lost sales and damaged customer relationships.

The electronics retailer employed various inventory manage-ment strategies to strike the right balance between carrying too much inventory and risking stockouts. First, they focused on accurate demand forecasting using historical sales data, industry trends, and market research. This allowed them to anticipate fluctuations in demand and adjust inventory levels accordingly. Additionally, they strengthened their relation-ships with suppliers, enabling them to negotiate favorable terms and ensure a consistent supply of goods even during periods of inflation.

By effectively adjusting prices and managing inventory levels during economic fluctuations, the electronics retailer was able to maintain profitability and continue to thrive despite challenging market conditions. This case study is a powerful example of how businesses can successfully navigate economic challenges by implementing the appropriate strategies and continuously monitoring market conditions.

To effectively manage inventory levels during economic fluc-tuations, retailers must employ a combination of practical strategies to ensure they maintain an optimal stock level. One fundamental aspect is accurate demand forecasting. By closely examining historical sales data, industry trends, and market re-search, businesses can anticipate changes in consumer demand and adjust their inventory accordingly. This proactive approach allows companies to be better prepared for shifts in the market, thereby minimizing the risk of overstocking or stockouts.

Another essential strategy for managing inventory levels is implementing just-in-time inventory systems. By maintaining leaner stock levels and ordering products as needed, businesses can reduce holding costs and avoid tying up capital in excess inventory. Just-in-time inventory systems rely on strong supplier relationships, efficient communication, and responsive logistics partners to function effectively. Therefore, establishing and nurturing these relationships is to successfully implement this approach.

Controlling costs during economic fluctuations is of equal significance for retailers. To maintain profitability, businesses must closely monitor and analyze their expenses, identifying areas where cost reductions can be made without compromising product quality or customer experience. By regularly reviewing their operational processes, overheads, and procurement arrangements, businesses can find opportunities to streamline operations and optimize resource allocation.

For instance, a company may discover that certain suppliers offer more competitive pricing or are willing to negotiate discounts based on volume or long-term commitments. By taking advantage of these opportunities, retailers can reduce their overall cost base while still providing high-quality products and services to their customers.

Effective inventory management and cost control are vital aspects of navigating economic fluctuations in the retail industry. By combining accurate demand forecasting, just-in-time inventory systems, and strong supplier relationships with diligent expense monitoring and analysis, businesses can position themselves for success and maintain profitability during periods of uncertainty. As we continue to explore the challenges and strategies associated with economic fluctuations, the next chapter will delve into the complexities of global supply chain management and guide us in overcoming potential obstacles.

To further illustrate the importance of cost control strategies, let us explore specific approaches that can be employed to maintain profitability during economic fluctuations. One such strategy involves renegotiating supplier contracts, which may result in more favorable terms and reduced business expenditures. By demonstrating loyalty and a history of prompt payments, companies stand a better chance at securing discounts, payment extensions, or other beneficial arrangements.

Another avenue for cost reduction lies in optimizing energy usage within business premises. This can be achieved by regularly maintaining heating, ventilation, and air conditioning systems, installing energy-efficient lighting, and encouraging employees to adopt energy-saving practices, such as turning off lights and equipment when not in use. These measures not only contribute to environmental sustainability but also lower utility expenses.

Streamlining operations is another aspect of cost control. Businesses can identify inefficiencies and redundancies contributing to unnecessary expenses by analyzing workflows, processes, and organizational structures. Eliminating these inefficiencies, consolidating tasks, and reorganizing teams can increase productivity and reduce operational costs.

Lastly, implementing technology solutions can significantly reduce labor expenses, one of many businesses' most significant cost drivers. Automation, artificial intelligence, and digital tools can improve efficiency, accuracy, and speed while reducing the need for extensive manual labor. However, balancing technological advancements and preserving the human touch that customers often appreciate is essential.

As an example of these cost control strategies in action, consider the case of Company X, a mid-sized retailer that faced severe challenges during a recent economic downturn. By adopting a multi-faceted approach to cost control, Company X was able to weather the storm and emerge stronger than before.

Company X began by renegotiating contracts with key suppliers, securing price reductions and more flexible payment terms. Concurrently, they invested in energy-efficient lighting, HVAC upgrades, and employee training to optimize energy consumption throughout their facilities. These improvements led to a 15% reduction in utility costs.

The company also conducted a thorough analysis of its operations, identifying inefficiencies and areas for improvement. By consolidating tasks, eliminating redundancies, and reorganizing teams, Company X increased productivity while reducing operational costs by 10%.

Lastly, Company X implemented technology solutions such as automation and AI-driven analytics to streamline processes and reduce labor expenses. These innovations enabled them to maintain customer service quality while reducing their workforce by 20%. By implementing these cost control strategies, Company X navigated the economic downturn successfully and sustained profitability.

This case study demonstrates the power of a comprehensive approach to cost control during challenging economic conditions. By employing a combination of supplier renegotiation, energy optimization, streamlined operations, and technology implementation, businesses can mitigate the impacts of economic fluctuations and maintain profitability. The next chapter will examine another aspect of navigating economic fluctuations: managing global supply chain challenges.

The importance of continuous monitoring and adjustment during economic fluctuations cannot be overstated. As businesses navigate the ebb and flow of market conditions, it is critical to stay vigilant and adapt strategies accordingly. One must regularly assess pricing, inventory, and cost control measures to ensure ongoing profitability, continually refining these tactics in response to changes in the economic landscape.

To successfully implement this approach, businesses should establish a process for routine analysis of their performance and market conditions. Reviewing financial statements, sales data, and industry trends on a monthly or quarterly basis can provide valuable insights into the effectiveness of current strategies and reveal areas that may require adjustments. By doing so, companies can proactively address potential challenges and capitalize on opportunities presented by economic fluctuations.

In summary, this chapter has highlighted several key strategies for maintaining profitability during economic fluctuations:

1. Adjusting prices: Businesses may need to consider lowering prices during a downturn to attract customers and maintain sales volume. Regularly conducting market research can help companies understand customer price sensitivity and competitor pricing strategies.

2. Managing inventory levels: During economic fluctuations, it is essential to manage inventory levels effectively, which can be achieved through accurate demand forecasting, implementing just-in-time inventory systems, and establishing strong supplier relationships.

3. Controlling costs: Closely monitoring and analyzing expenses can identify areas where cost reductions can be made without compromising product quality or customer experience. Specific cost control strategies discussed include renegotiating supplier contracts, optimizing energy usage, streamlining operations, and implementing technology solutions to reduce labor costs.

By embracing these strategies, businesses can better navigate the challenges of economic fluctuations and ultimately achieve sustained success. Through diligence, adaptability, and a constant drive for improvement, companies can continue to thrive even amidst uncertainty.

As we move forward, we will explore the complexities of operating in an ever-changing economic environment. The next chapter will focus on managing global supply chain challenges during economic fluctuations, providing additional insights and strategies for maintaining profitability in adversity.

Adapting to economic fluctuations is vital for any business seeking long-term success. As we have seen throughout this chapter, implementing the strategies outlined - adjusting prices, managing inventory levels, and controlling costs - will enable organizations to navigate these challenges effectively. By regularly assessing and adapting their operations based on market conditions, businesses can maintain their profitability even during uncertain times.

Adapting in the face of economic change cannot be understated. Companies can confidently weather the storm of financial instability through a proactive approach that combines market research, effective inventory management, and cost control measures. The examples provided in this chapter serve as a testament to these strategies' effectiveness and should inspire readers' confidence that they, too, can successfully navigate the challenges posed by economic fluctuations.

Our next area of focus will be navigating global supply chain challenges during economic fluctuations. This topic is especially relevant in today's interconnected world, where companies often rely on networks across countries and continents. By examining the intricacies of managing global supply chains in the face of economic ups and downs, we will provide valuable insights and practical guidance for businesses looking to optimize their operations and maintain profitability amidst unpredictable circumstances.

Navigating Global Supply Chain Challenges

The retail industry is a complex web of interconnected businesses and suppliers working in unison to deliver products to the end consumer. This intricate network is susceptible to various global supply chain challenges that can cause significant disruptions to business operations. These challenges can range from natural disasters, such as earthquakes or hurricanes, which can destroy critical infrastructure; political instability, leading to sudden changes in regulations or trade policies; trade disputes, resulting in tariffs or embargoes; or even pandemics, which can upend normal business operations worldwide.

Understanding the potential impact of these disruptions is for retailers, as they rely heavily on their supply chains to meet customer demands and maintain profitability. When faced with such challenges, the consequences can be severe. For instance, delays in product delivery may lead to lost sales, while increased costs stemming from supply chain issues can eat into profit margins. Additionally, inventory shortages caused by disruptions can result in stockouts, further damaging customer satisfaction and brand reputation.

We have witnessed numerous real-world examples of global supply chain disruptions impacting retail businesses in recent history. One notable instance was the 2011 Tohoku earthquake and tsunami in Japan, which caused immense destruction locally and disrupted global supply chains across various industries, including electronics and automotive sectors. Retailers relying on components and products from affected regions faced delivery delays, forcing them to scramble for alternative sources, often at higher costs.

Similarly, the ongoing trade dispute between the United States and China has profoundly impacted numerous businesses, including those in the retail sector. With both countries imposing tariffs on each other's goods, retailers have grappled with increased costs for imported products, leading to higher consumer prices or reduced business profit margins. In some cases, companies have been forced to shift their production or sourcing strategies to mitigate the effects of these trade tensions.

Understanding the significance of global supply chain challenges and their potential impact on retail businesses is paramount for success in this industry. By recognizing the various disruptions that may occur, retailers can better prepare themselves to navigate these challenges and maintain their competitive edge in an increasingly globalized market.

Given the potential for disruptions in global supply chains, as illustrated by the examples provided earlier, it becomes increasingly important for retail businesses to adopt risk management and contingency planning strategies. These approaches enable companies to anticipate and respond effectively to challenges, minimizing disruptions and maintaining a competitive edge.

Risk management involves identifying potential risks, assessing their impact, and developing mitigation strategies. Retailers can begin by systematically evaluating their supply chains to pinpoint vulnerabilities, such as single points of failure, supplier concentration, or overreliance on specific regions. By conducting regular risk assessments, businesses can stay informed about emerging threats and proactively address them before they escalate into a full-blown crisis.

Contingency planning is complementary by outlining a company's steps during a supply chain disruption. This may include alternative sourcing arrangements, inventory management adjustments, or logistical changes. A well-crafted contingency plan provides a roadmap for navigating unforeseen challenges, ensuring that retailers can maintain operations and minimize negative impacts on customers and revenue streams.

In addition to risk management and contingency planning, diversifying suppliers is another key strategy for managing supply chain risks. By working with multiple suppliers, retailers reduce their dependence on a single source, lessening the impact of disruptions from one particular supplier. This approach also increases flexibility in sourcing materials or products, allowing businesses to adapt more quickly to changing market conditions or evolving customer demands.

Furthermore, engaging with a diverse range of suppliers can stimulate innovation and drive improvements in product quality as suppliers compete for business and strive to differentiate themselves. This competition ultimately benefits the retailer, fostering an environment conducive to continuous improvement and value creation.

In summary, navigating global supply chain challenges requires retailers to adopt a proactive stance, focusing on risk management, contingency planning, and supplier diversification. By implementing these strategies, businesses can better prepare for potential disruptions, mitigate their impact, and maintain a competitive advantage in an increasingly complex and interconnected global marketplace.

Building strong relationships between retailers and suppliers is critical to maintaining a resilient supply chain. One notable example of such a successful partnership can be found in the collaboration between a prominent sportswear retailer and its network of fabric suppliers. Through open communication, trust, and a shared commitment to innovation, they were able to jointly develop a cutting-edge, sustainable material that set them apart from competitors.

This alliance demonstrates the importance of collaboration in fostering innovation and driving efficiencies across the supply chain. By working closely with their suppliers, the sportswear retailer gained valuable insights into new production techniques, which allowed them to stay ahead of industry trends and meet growing consumer demand for eco-friendly products.

Furthermore, open communication and trust are vital components of these successful partnerships. When retailers and suppliers share information transparently and communicate regularly about challenges, opportunities, and expectations, they can better anticipate potential disruptions and collaboratively find solutions. This ongoing dialogue helps build trust, which is essential for developing long-term, mutually beneficial relationships.

In addition to solid relationships, technology plays an increasingly important role in managing global supply chain challenges. Retailers have access to various supply chain technologies designed to enhance efficiency, reduce costs, and improve visibility across their operations. For example, inventory management systems can help retailers track stock levels in real time, enabling them to optimize replenishment processes and reduce the risk of stockouts or excess inventory.

Demand forecasting tools are another valuable resource for retailers, as they use historical sales data and market trends to predict future demand patterns. This information allows businesses to make informed decisions about when and how much to order from suppliers, minimizing the risk of overstocking or understocking certain items.

Logistics optimization software is also in managing global supply chain challenges. These sophisticated applications consider shipping routes, transportation modes, and lead times to help retailers identify the most cost-effective and efficient way to transport goods from suppliers to distribution centers or stores.

Incorporating these technologies into supply chain management strategies can significantly improve efficiency and cost reduction. For instance, implementing an advanced inventory management system allowed a major electronics retailer to reduce inventory levels by 20%, leading to substantial savings on warehousing costs.

Building strong relationships with suppliers and leveraging technology are essential to navigating global supply chain challenges. Retailers that prioritize collaboration, open communication, trust in their supplier partnerships, and invest in cutting-edge supply chain technologies will be better equipped to manage potential disruptions and maintain a competitive edge in the ever-evolving retail landscape.

Implementing a risk management plan for global supply chain challenges is paramount for retailers striving to maintain a competitive edge in an increasingly complex business landscape. The first step in this process involves conducting a comprehensive risk assessment, which entails identifying potential threats to the supply chain and evaluating their likelihood of occurrence and potential impact on operations. This may include natural disasters, political instability, trade disputes, or pandemics.

Once these risks have been identified and assessed, retailers must develop contingency plans to mitigate their effects. These plans should outline specific actions that can be taken to minimize disruptions, such as finding alternative sources of materials, adjusting production schedules, or implementing backup logistics arrangements. For example, a retailer facing the risk of disturbance due to a natural disaster might establish secondary suppliers in different geographic locations to ensure continuity of supply in case of emergency.

Establishing communication channels with suppliers is also in managing supply chain risks effectively. Retailers should maintain open lines of communication with their supplier network to facilitate the timely sharing of information, enabling both parties to respond promptly and appropriately to any emerging issues. Regular meetings, conference calls, and email updates are some examples of methods that can be employed to foster ongoing dialogue and collaboration between retailers and suppliers.

Diversifying suppliers is another essential strategy in mitigating supply chain risks.

Retailers can reduce their dependence on a single source by working with multiple suppliers, thereby increasing flexibility in sourcing materials or products. To do this effectively, businesses must conduct thorough supplier evaluations considering quality, reliability, lead times, and pricing factors. By gathering data on these aspects, retailers can decide which suppliers to partner with and how to allocate their purchasing volumes.

Negotiating contracts with multiple suppliers is also essential in managing risks effectively. Retailers should negotiate favorable terms that provide flexibility and minimize potential disruptions, including clauses that address lead times, order quantities, and contingencies for unforeseen events. Additionally, businesses should be prepared to renegotiate contracts to adapt to changing market conditions or supplier performance.

Regularly reviewing and updating supplier relationships is another critical aspect of diversifying suppliers effectively. Retailers should continuously monitor the performance of their suppliers and make adjustments as necessary to ensure they are working with the most reliable and cost-effective partners. This may involve revisiting supplier evaluations, renegotiating contracts, or seeking new suppliers to replace underperforming ones.

By implementing a risk management plan that includes conducting risk assessments, developing contingency plans, establishing communication channels, and diversifying suppliers, retailers can better navigate global supply chain challenges and minimize disruptions to their operations. These proactive measures will ultimately contribute to maintaining profitability and business continuity in an ever-changing retail landscape.

Monitoring and evaluating supply chain performance is paramount for retailers to optimize their operations. One way to assess the effectiveness of supply chain management strategies is by tracking key performance indicators (KPIs). These critical metrics provide insights into various aspects of a retailer's supply chain, enabling them to make data-driven decisions that enhance efficiency and mitigate risks.

One such KPI is the on-time delivery rate, which measures the percentage of shipments that arrive within the agreed-upon time frame. Retailers can use this metric to gauge the reliability of their suppliers' reliability and identify areas where improvements can be made to ensure timely deliveries. High on-time delivery rates are for maintaining customer satisfaction and avoiding stockouts.

Inventory turnover is another important KPI, as it represents the number of times inventory is sold or used during a specific period. A high inventory turnover rate indicates that a retailer is efficiently managing its stock levels and minimizing carrying costs, while a low rate may signal overstocking or issues with product demand. By monitoring inventory turnover, retailers can better align their purchasing and sales strategies, ultimately improving profitability.

In today's digital age, investing in supply chain technologies offers numerous benefits for retail businesses. These advanced tools can streamline processes, improve visibility across the supply chain, and bolster overall resilience in the face of global challenges. For example, inventory management systems enable retailers to track stock levels in real-time, allowing for more accurate replenishment planning and reducing the risk of stockouts.

On the other hand, demand forecasting tools utilize historical sales data and sophisticated algorithms to predict future product demand. By leveraging these insights, retailers can optimize their inventory levels, identify potential sales opportunities, and reduce the likelihood of excess stock.

Lastly, logistics optimization software can support retailers in identifying the most efficient shipping routes and transportation methods, minimizing delivery times and costs. This enhances customer satisfaction and contributes to a more sustainable and environmentally friendly supply chain.

Monitoring and evaluating supply chain performance through KPIs such as on-time delivery rates and inventory turnover is essential for retailers to optimize their operations. Additionally, investing in supply chain technologies can further streamline processes, enhance visibility, and improve overall resilience, helping retail businesses navigate the complex landscape of global supply chain challenges.

Several retail businesses have demonstrated the effectiveness of proactive supply chain management in overcoming global challenges. These success stories serve as valuable examples for others looking to navigate the complex landscape of supply chain disruptions.

One notable example is a prominent sportswear retailer that faced significant delays in product delivery due to ongoing trade disputes. By implementing a diversified supplier strategy, the company could source materials from multiple suppliers in different regions, reducing its dependence on any single source. This approach allowed the retailer to maintain consistent product availability and minimize the impact of geopolitical tensions on its operations.

Another inspiring case study involves a leading electronics retailer successfully mitigating the risks of a sudden factory shutdown in one of its key manufacturing locations. The company had previously identified this potential risk and developed contingency plans, which included securing alternative production facilities and maintaining open communication channels with suppliers. When the shutdown occurred, the retailer swiftly executed its backup plan, ensuring minimal product availability and customer satisfaction disruption.

These examples highlight the importance of proactive planning and adapting to the ever-changing global supply chain landscape. Retailers that can identify potential risks, assess their impact, and develop effective mitigation strategies are better positioned to weather the storm of disruptions and maintain profitability.

Facing global supply chain challenges requires retailers to prioritize risk management and contingency planning. By diversifying suppliers, building strong relationships, investing in technology, and monitoring performance indicators, businesses can mitigate the adverse effects of disruptions and maintain a resilient supply chain.

Retailers must be proactive and diligent in their supply chain management efforts, learning from the successes of others and applying these insights to their operations. By doing so, they safeguard their profitability and contribute to a more sustainable and robust global retail industry.

A wealth of resources is available for readers seeking to expand their understanding of global supply chain challenges and delve further into risk mitigation strategies. These resources will enable you to develop a more comprehensive view of the topic, offering expert insights and practical guidance for navigating the complex world of supply chain management.

Several books stand out as essential reads for anyone interested in exploring this subject in greater depth. "The Resilient

Enterprise" by Yossi Sheffi provides a comprehensive analysis of supply chain risks and offers actionable advice on how businesses can enhance their resilience in the face of disruptions. Similarly, "Global Supply Chain Ecosystems" by Mark Millar provides valuable perspectives on the interconnected nature of global supply chains and discusses strategies for managing risks and optimizing performance.

In addition to these books, numerous articles and research papers offer insights into retail businesses' challenges in today's globalized economy. The Harvard Business Review, for instance, regularly publishes articles on supply chain management, risk assessment, and contingency planning. A simple search on their website will yield a treasure trove of information on these topics. Additionally, leading industry publications such as Supply Chain Management Review and Industry Week frequently cover issues related to global supply chain challenges and best practices for overcoming them.

Websites dedicated to supply chain management and risk mitigation can provide valuable information and up-to-date news on emerging trends and challenges. Some notable examples include the Council of Supply Chain Management Professionals (CSCMP) and the Global Supply Chain Institute (GSCI). These organizations offer a wealth of resources, including whitepapers, webinars, and conferences, aimed at helping businesses navigate the ever-evolving landscape of global supply chains.

To ensure a coherent narrative throughout this chapter, we have carefully examined the presented ideas and maintained a consistent focus on navigating global supply chain challenges.

Including real-world examples, case studies, and supplementary resources has provided readers with an engaging and informative exploration of this complex subject. Combined with the additional resources provided in this scene, the guidance offered within this chapter will equip readers with the tools necessary to manage supply chain risks effectively and maintain a resilient retail business.

In summary, by combining the strategies and insights discussed in this chapter with further exploration of recommended resources, retailers can develop a deeper understanding of global supply chain challenges and confidently implement risk mitigation measures. Through proactive management, businesses can enhance their resilience, adapt to disruptions, and safeguard long-term profitability.

Regulatory Changes and Profit Margins

L et's examine some real-world examples to grasp the practical implications of regulatory changes fully. One notable instance is the tariffs imposed on imported goods, which can drastically increase the cost of obtaining products from overseas suppliers. In 2018, the United States implemented tariffs on various goods imported from China, causing many retailers to reevaluate their sourcing strategies. Companies like Walmart and Target faced higher costs for products ranging from electronics to clothing, leading some to explore alternative suppliers or pass the added expenses onto consumers through increased prices.

Another example of regulatory changes impacting retailers involves shifts in tax policies.

Governments may introduce new taxes or modify existing ones to raise revenue or stimulate economic growth. For instance, when the European Union implemented the Value-Added Tax (VAT) system, retailers had to adjust their pricing structures to include this additional tax, ultimately affecting their profit margins. Furthermore, changes in corporate tax rates can directly affect a retailer's overall profitability.

Lastly, new labor regulations are another type of regulatory change that can significantly impact wage costs for retailers. A prime example is the gradual increase in minimum wage across numerous regions worldwide. As governments aim to improve living standards for workers, businesses, including retailers, must absorb these higher labor costs or find ways to offset them through operational efficiencies or price adjustments.

Introducing mandatory employee benefits, such as healthcare or parental leave, can also increase retailers' costs, necessitating strategic adaptations to protect profit margins.

Examining these real-world examples makes it clear that regulatory changes can have far-reaching effects on retail businesses. Staying informed about these adjustments and understanding their potential impact on profit margins is for retailers in today's ever-evolving regulatory landscape.

Considering the potential impact of regulatory changes on retail profit margins, staying informed cannot be overstated. Retailers must make a conscious effort to monitor industry news and updates regularly. This can involve subscribing to newsletters or engaging in online forums where professionals discuss current events and their implications on the sector. By keeping a finger on the pulse of regulatory shifts, retailers can prepare for any potential challenges and adjust their strategies accordingly.

In addition to monitoring industry news, joining relevant trade associations or professional networks can prove invaluable for staying informed about regulatory changes. Such organizations often provide resources and insights tailored to their members' needs. They may also host conferences, workshops, or webinars that address emerging regulatory issues, offering valuable opportunities for learning and networking with other professionals facing similar challenges.

Establishing relationships with legal or regulatory experts is another aspect of staying informed about regulatory changes. Lawyers, consultants, and other professionals specializing in the retail sector can offer guidance on navigating complex regulations and ensuring compliance. By building a team of knowledgeable advisors, retailers can more effectively anticipate and respond to regulatory developments.

There are numerous resources available to help retailers stay informed about regulatory changes. Industry publications like trade magazines or journals often feature articles analyzing recent regulatory shifts and their business implications. Government websites also serve as essential sources of information, as they typically publish official notices and updates on regulatory changes, including detailed explanations of new requirements or deadlines. Legal advisors specializing in retail law can provide updates and insights on regulatory developments, helping retailers understand the potential impact on their operations and guiding them through adaptation and compliance.

Staying informed about regulatory changes is vital for retailers aiming to protect their profit margins and ensure compliance with evolving requirements. By regularly monitoring industry news, joining trade associations or professional networks, and establishing relationships with legal or regulatory experts, retailers can better navigate the complex world of regulations and position themselves for long-term success.

Failing to comply with regulatory requirements can lead to severe consequences for retailers. The financial risks involved can be substantial, as non-compliance often results in hefty fines and penalties that can significantly impact a retailer's bottom line.

Moreover, these costs can escalate if the issue is not addressed promptly or if multiple violations are identified.

Reputational risks are also a significant concern for non-compliant retailers. In today's highly connected world, news of regulatory breaches can spread quickly, leading to negative publicity and damage to a company's brand image. This, in turn, may result in decreased customer trust and loyalty, ultimately affecting sales and market share.

Retailers must recognize non-compliance potential risks and consequences and prioritize regulatory adherence in their business operations.

Retailers must adapt their pricing strategies to protect profit margins in the face of regulatory changes. One practical approach is to conduct regular pricing reviews, assessing the potential impact of regulatory changes on costs and pricing structures. By closely monitoring the evolving regulatory land-scape and adjusting prices as needed, retailers can maintain profitability while ensuring compliance with new regulations.

In conducting these pricing reviews, retailers should consider various factors, including the effect of tariffs on imported goods, changes in tax policies, and any new labor regulations that may impact wage costs. By thoroughly evaluating the specific implications of each regulatory change, retailers can make informed decisions about adjusting their pricing strategies to safeguard profit margins.

Additionally, retailers should explore cost-saving measures that can help offset the increased expenses resulting from regulatory changes. For example, they may seek out alternative suppliers, renegotiate contracts to secure more favorable terms or invest in technologies that streamline operations and reduce overhead costs. By proactively identifying opportunities to improve efficiency and lower costs, retailers can better position themselves to weather the challenges posed by regulatory shifts.

In summary, understanding and addressing the potential risks and consequences of non-compliance with regulatory requirements is essential for retailers seeking to protect their profit margins and maintain a positive brand image. By conducting regular pricing reviews, assessing the impact of regulatory changes on costs and pricing structures, and exploring cost-saving measures, retailers can adapt their pricing strategies to ensure compliance and preserve profitability in an ever-changing regulatory landscape.

As retailers navigate regulatory challenges, staying informed about the specific requirements and implications of any regulation changes is . This knowledge enables businesses to make well-informed decisions and take necessary actions to mitigate potential adverse effects on their operations.

One effective approach for addressing regulatory challenges is adjusting sourcing options or supply chain strategies to reduce the impact of tariffs or taxes. For instance, retailers could consider diversifying their supplier base by working with vendors from multiple countries or regions, thereby reducing the risk associated with any single supplier or region facing higher tariffs. Furthermore, exploring local or domestic suppliers could minimize exposure to import duties or currency fluctuations.

Another key aspect of navigating regulatory challenges is optimizing supply chain logistics. Retailers may benefit from investing in technology solutions that improve inventory management and streamline the flow of goods through the supply chain, minimizing delays or bottlenecks that could lead to increased costs. By enhancing their supply chain efficiency, retailers can better manage the cost implications of regulatory changes.

Emphasizing the importance of compliance with regulatory requirements cannot be overstated. Failing to comply with these rules can result in severe financial consequences, such as fines and penalties, as well as reputational damage, which can have long-lasting impacts on a business's success. To ensure compliance, retailers must monitor regulatory changes and adapt their practices accordingly.

A proactive approach to compliance involves staying informed about upcoming regulatory changes, assessing their potential impact on business operations, and implementing necessary adjustments in a timely manner. This could include updating internal policies, providing employee training on new regulations, or seeking external expertise to help navigate complex legal requirements.

Effective navigating regulatory challenges requires understanding regulatory changes' specific requirements and implications, exploring alternative sourcing options or supply chain strategies, and maintaining compliance while safeguarding profit margins. By staying informed, proactive, and adaptable, retailers can successfully manage the ever-evolving regulatory landscape, ensuring the longevity and success of their businesses.

Establishing relationships with legal or regulatory experts is to ensure compliance and navigate the complex landscape of regulations in retail. These professionals possess specialized knowledge and experience in dealing with regulatory matters, making them valuable resources for retailers to rely on when faced with challenging regulatory changes.

By working closely with legal and regulatory advisors, retailers can gain insights into the intricacies of new regulations, identify potential areas of non-compliance, and develop strategies to address these issues proactively. Furthermore, these experts can help retailers stay updated on any changes in regulations that may affect their businesses so they can make informed decisions and avoid costly mistakes.

In addition to seeking professional advice when needed, retailers should also consider joining industry associations or networking groups, which often provide access to valuable resources like webinars, workshops, and newsletters focused on regulatory updates and best practices for compliance. Through these channels, retailers can expand their knowledge base and connect with peers facing similar challenges, fostering a collaborative approach to overcoming regulatory hurdles.

To illustrate the point further, let us look at some examples of retailers successfully adapting their pricing strategies in response to regulatory changes while protecting their profit margins. One such example is a major electronics retailer that faced increased import tariffs on certain products. By leveraging data analytics and carefully examining their product assortment, the company identified alternative sourcing options that minimized the impact of the tariffs on their cost structure.

Another example is a clothing retailer that had to navigate changes in labor regulations, resulting in increased wage costs. In response, the company restructured its pricing strategy by conducting regular competitive price analyses and identifying opportunities to optimize its product mix, focusing on higher-margin items to offset the rise in labor expenses. As a result, the retailer was able to maintain its profitability while remaining compliant with the new labor laws.

These case studies demonstrate that, with careful planning and strategic thinking, retailers can adapt to regulatory changes without sacrificing profit margins. By staying informed, seeking professional advice, and continually reassessing their pricing strategies, retailers can successfully navigate the ever-changing world of regulations while ensuring the long-term success of their businesses.

By adapting pricing strategies to comply with regulatory changes, retailers can unlock several long-term benefits contributing to their overall success. One such benefit is maintaining a competitive edge in the market. When retailers proactively adjust their pricing strategies according to new regulations, they understand the current market dynamics and showcase their agility in responding to these shifts. This level of responsiveness can make a significant difference in standing out against competitors who may need to react or be more informed about regulatory developments.

Another advantage of staying informed and proactive in adjusting pricing strategies is the potential to build trust with customers. Consumers appreciate businesses that prioritize compliance and uphold ethical standards. Demonstrating transparency and adherence to regulations communicates a commitment to responsible business practices, which can foster customer loyalty and enhance brand reputation.

It is for retailers to stay vigilant when it comes to monitoring regulatory changes and understanding the potential impact on their profit margins. By doing so, they can adapt their pricing strategies accordingly and ensure compliance with regulatory requirements. The key takeaways from this chapter are:

- Stay informed about regulatory changes and their potential impact on retail profit margins.
- Seek professional advice when needed and establish relationships with legal or regulatory experts.
- Regularly assess the potential impact of regulatory changes on costs and pricing structures.
- Adjust sourcing options or supply chain strategies to mitigate the effects of tariffs or taxes.
- Maintain compliance with regulatory requirements while safeguarding profit margins.

By embracing these principles, retailers can successfully navigate the complex landscape of regulations and build a solid foundation for their businesses. Adapting pricing strategies protects profit margins, helps maintain a competitive edge, and fosters trust with customers, ensuring their retail operations' long-term success and sustainability.

Emerging Trends in Retail

The retail landscape is continuously shaped by emerging trends that influence consumer behaviors, market dynamics, and the competitive environment. By staying informed and adapting quickly, retailers can capitalize on these trends to boost profit margins and sustain long-term success.

This chapter provides an in-depth look at key retail trends, including omnichannel retailing, personalization, automation, and sustainability. We analyze real-world examples of retailers benefiting from these trends while offering research-backed recommendations on implementation strategies. The insights aim to equip retail businesses with the knowledge to embrace innovation, meet evolving consumer demands, and ultimately enhance profitability.

Omnichannel Retailing: Unifying the Customer Experience

Omnichannel retailing involves tightly integrating online, mobile, and brick-and-mortar channels to deliver seamless shopping journeys. Customers can fluidly research, purchase, collect, or return items across touchpoints while enjoying consistent brand interactions. Forrester reports that omnichannel customers have 30% higher lifetime value than those using just one channel.

Retail giants like Walmart and Amazon have invested heavily in omnichannel capabilities, allowing customers to move effort-lessly between browsing online and visiting physical stores. A Harvard study found omnichannel customers spend 4% more per in-store trip and 10% more per online order compared to single-channel shoppers. By providing unified experiences, retailers boost convenience, satisfaction, and ultimately sales.

Recommendations for Implementation:

- Invest in unified commerce platforms linking inventory, CRM, and order/delivery data.
- Allow customers to purchase online and collect instore or vice versa.
- Share order histories and personalized promotions across channels.
- Offer consistent pricing and discounts online and offline.

Personalization: Targeting Individual Shopper Preferences

Personalization involves customizing product assortments, recommendations, promotions and overall shopping experi-ences to match individual consumer preferences and behaviors. Sophisticated algorithms analyze purchase history and brows-ing data to derive shopper insights. 72% of customers only engage with personalized messaging, per Epsilon research.

Starbucks rewards members receive tailored bonuses and discounts via its mobile app based on their previous orders. Fashion retailer Stitchfix applies personalization exceptionally by having customers fill out detailed style quizzes. Each user then receives a personalized shipment of clothing items curated by a stylist. 72% of customers feel the service meets their style and budget preferences accurately.

Recommendations for Implementation:

- Incentivize customers to share personal preference details via quizzes or questionnaires.
- Track online browsing behaviors using cookies and recommend related or recently viewed items.
- Show personalized promotions and recommended products aligned to purchase history data.
- Segment customers into groups by behavior and tailor messaging accordingly.

Automation: Improving Efficiency and Reducing Costs

Automating repetitive tasks with technologies like artificial intelligence, predictive analytics, IoT sensors and robotics promises significant value. Self-checkout systems enable customers to scan purchases autonomously, reducing labor costs. Warehouse robotics and automated inventory replenishment boost supply chain efficiencies. chatbots resolve customer queries 24/7 without human agents.

Home Depot's warehouse automation systems have improved

picking speed by 20% and accuracy by 25% while lowering labor expenses. Cosmetics retailer Sephora implemented AI-powered recommendation engines which increased sales of suggested products by 10-15%. Automation empowers retailers to operate more productively and steer savings into profit growth.

Recommendations for Implementation:

- Install self-checkout options across brick-and-mortar stores to empower customer autonomy.
- Adopt warehouse automation solutions to optimize fulfillment, inventory, and shipping operations.
- Test conversational chatbots or kiosks to handle basic customer service queries independently.
- Develop algorithms that analyze POS and inventory data to optimize future demand planning.

Sustainability: Satisfying Eco-Conscious Consumers

With 92% of consumers concerned about environmental impact, sustainable practices are now mainstream customer expectations. Product lifecycle assessments reveal packaging accounts for 20-45% of retailers' environmental impact. Eliminating unnecessary plastics and shifting to recycled or renewable materials caters to eco-aware shoppers. BASF reports 63% of consumers are even willing to pay 10% or more for sustainable products, underlining this segment's profit potential.

Outdoor apparel retailer Patagonia has put environmental stewardship at the core of its brand ethos. Through sustainable materials sourcing, implementing product recycling schemes, powering facilities via renewable energy and streamlining packaging, Patagonia makes eco-friendly choices accessible to customers at every touchpoint.

Recommendations for Implementation:

- Conduct audits to identify sustainability hotspots across the product lifecycle.
- Set incremental targets to reduce waste, emissions, water use and power consumption annually.
- Train employees as brand ambassadors for sustainability programs and messaging.
- Promote green credentials clearly in-store and online to capitalize on conscious consumer demand.

In closing, capitalizing on emerging experience-enhancing and efficiency-driving trends in retail enables enduring relevance, growth and profitability through changing market landscapes. We encourage you to apply these insights by continually monitoring the retail horizon, testing innovative concepts, and integrating impactful developments into your operational frameworks and strategic roadmaps. The winner in modern retail is not the largest or strongest but the most adaptable and forward-looking. By embracing that mindset and using this chapter as your guide, your business can remain competitively positioned to maximize profit margins both now and for years to come.

Sustainability and Pricing

To understand the significance of sustainability in retail, it is essential first to define the concept itself. At its core, sustainability encompasses three fundamental dimensions:

1. Environmental
2. Social
3. Economic Considerations

The ecological aspect refers to preserving and protecting our planet's natural resources, minimizing waste, reducing pollution, and combating climate change. Social sustainability involves promoting fair labor practices, fostering inclusive communities, and prioritizing health and well-being for all. Lastly, the economic dimension focuses on creating long-term value through responsible resource management, investing in sustainable growth, and ensuring financial stability.

In the context of the retail industry, sustainability transcends mere buzzwords or marketing tactics; it represents a comprehensive approach to doing business that considers the dimensions above. By embracing sustainable practices, retailers can cater to the evolving preferences of environmentally conscious customers and contribute to developing a more sustainable future. This shift presents opportunities and challenges, necessitating a careful examination of existing business models and a willingness to innovate and adapt.

Addressing the environmental impact of products and services is paramount for businesses adopting sustainable practices. The shift towards sustainability meets the ever-growing consumer demand for eco-friendly options and encourages businesses to reevaluate their pricing strategies in light of these concerns. By considering the ecological footprint of their offerings, companies can make informed decisions about pricing that reflect both the financial and non-financial value they provide to customers.

Sustainability affects pricing decisions by requiring businesses to account for the costs associated with environmentally responsible production methods, materials sourcing, and waste management. These factors can influence a product's overall value proposition as consumers increasingly prioritize ethical and eco-conscious choices over those that may be cheaper but less sustainable in the long run. Consequently, businesses must balance competitive pricing and promote sustainable practices to remain relevant in today's market.

Businesses can implement various strategies to integrate sustainable practices into their pricing models. One approach is to offer eco-friendly products or services at a premium price, reflecting the added value and cost associated with sustainability efforts. This tactic acknowledges the higher expenses often incurred using sustainable materials, energy-efficient production processes, and other environmentally conscious measures. By charging a premium for such offerings, businesses can help consumers understand the actual cost of sustainability and encourage them to invest in products that contribute to a greener future.

Another method for incorporating sustainability into pricing structures involves utilizing incentives or discounts for customers who engage in eco-friendly behaviors. For instance, businesses might reward patrons who bring reusable bags, return packaging materials for reuse, or participate in recycling programs. Such initiatives can help reinforce a company's sustainability commitment while fostering customer loyalty and goodwill.

In summary, the integration of sustainable practices into business operations necessitates a thorough examination of pricing strategies. Companies must consider the environmental impact of their products and services and communicate the value of sustainability to customers through pricing adjustments and promotional efforts. By doing so, businesses can successfully navigate the challenges and seize the opportunities associated with the growing demand for eco-friendly retail options.

To better understand the implementation of sustainable pricing strategies, let us examine some practical examples and case studies of businesses that have successfully applied these approaches in their operations.

Patagonia, an outdoor clothing and gear brand, is one of the most well-known companies to adopt a sustainable pricing strategy. Patagonia's commitment to environmental responsibility is evident in its use of recycled materials, fair trade labor practices, and investment in renewable energy. As part of its strategy, the company prices its products at a premium, reflecting the added value of these sustainable practices. Consumers are drawn to Patagonia's offerings despite the higher cost due to their quality and unwavering dedication to protecting the environment. Amid the challenges of balancing sustainability and profitability, Patagonia has thrived, demonstrating the positive outcomes achievable through sustainable pricing.

In another example, Tesla, the electric vehicle manufacturer, has employed a dynamic pricing model designed to account for the actual cost of producing its innovative, eco-friendly vehicles. While Tesla's cars initially carried a higher price tag than traditional gasoline-fueled vehicles, the company strategically lowered prices over time as production costs decreased and economies of scale were realized. This approach allowed Tesla to maintain its sustainability commitment and made electric vehicles more accessible to a broader customer base.

By implementing sustainable pricing strategies, businesses can reap numerous benefits.

Attracting environmentally conscious customers is one such advantage, as evidenced by both Patagonia and Tesla. Consumers who prioritize sustainability are often willing to pay a premium for products and services that align with their values, ultimately contributing to increased revenue and long-term customer loyalty.

Additionally, sustainable pricing can enhance a company's brand reputation. As businesses increasingly face scrutiny from customers, investors, and regulators alike, incorporating sustainability into pricing models demonstrates a commitment to social and environmental responsibility. This can lead to greater stakeholder trust and credibility, helping businesses stand out in a crowded marketplace.

Most significantly, sustainable pricing strategies contribute to a more sustainable future. By incorporating the costs associated with environmentally responsible practices and materials into product pricing, businesses can help shift consumer behavior towards eco-friendly choices. This, in turn, drives innovation and investment in sustainable technologies and practices, ultimately fostering a greener economy for all.

Practical examples from companies like Patagonia and Tesla illustrate the potential success achievable by implementing sustainable pricing strategies. Despite the challenges faced, these businesses have balanced profitability and environmental responsibility, enjoying the benefits of enhanced brand reputation and customer loyalty. As we progress, more companies must consider adopting sustainable pricing models to secure long-term success and contribute to a more environmentally conscious future.

While the benefits of sustainable pricing are clear, it is essential to acknowledge and address potential concerns or objections that businesses may have. One such concern is the possible increased costs associated with implementing sustainable practices. These additional expenses can stem from sourcing eco-friendly materials, upgrading manufacturing processes, or investing in renewable energy sources.

To overcome this challenge, businesses can explore various cost-saving measures and innovative solutions. For instance, they can invest in energy-efficient equipment, which, although initially more expensive, can lead to long-term savings on energy bills. Businesses can also collaborate with suppliers with similar sustainability goals, thereby negotiating better prices for eco-friendly materials.

Another concern is potential customer resistance to higher-priced sustainable products or services. While there is a growing demand for environmentally friendly options, some consumers may hesitate to pay a premium. To address this, businesses must emphasize the value proposition of their sustainably priced products or services. This can be achieved by high-lighting the tangible benefits – such as durability, efficiency, or improved health outcomes – customers can expect from choosing eco-friendly options.

This brings us to the importance of transparency and communi-cation in sustainable pricing. Businesses need to communicate the environmental benefits of their products or services to customers. In doing so, they educate consumers about the impacts of their purchasing decisions and justify any price premiums associated with sustainable offerings.

One effective way to communicate the environmental benefits

of a product or service is through storytelling. By sharing the story behind sustainable practices, businesses can connect emotionally with customers, inspiring them to make more environmentally conscious choices. This narrative should be supported by factual information, such as carbon footprint reduction or water conservation data, to solidify the credibility of the business's sustainability claims.

Furthermore, businesses can leverage digital platforms and marketing channels to spread their message. For example, they can create engaging content – such as blog posts, videos, or infographics – that demonstrates their commitment to sustainability, showcases the positive impacts of their products or services, and encourages consumers to join them in their journey towards a more sustainable future.

Addressing potential concerns about sustainable pricing and effectively communicating the environmental benefits of products and services are for businesses seeking to adopt this strategy. By overcoming these challenges and embracing transparency, companies can foster consumer trust, enhance brand reputation, and ultimately contribute to a greener, more sustainable world.

Certifications and labels hold a significant role in sustainable pricing, as they validate a business's commitment to eco-friendly practices and instill confidence in consumers.

These certifications, such as organic or fair trade labels, act as a seal of approval, assuring customers that a product has met stringent criteria and adheres to specific environmental, social, and ethical standards.

To obtain these certifications, businesses must undergo a comprehensive evaluation process by third-party organizations. This assessment examines various aspects of a company's operations, from sourcing materials and ingredients to production processes and labor practices. By securing these certifications, businesses can showcase their dedication to sustainability, strengthening their reputation and justifying any premium prices associated with their eco-friendly offerings.

In addition to certifications, collaboration and partnerships are vital components in implementing sustainable pricing strategies. Businesses can pool resources, share knowledge, and enhance their collective impact on sustainability efforts by forging alliances with like-minded suppliers, organizations, or even competitors. These collaborations can take many forms, from co-developing new products and technologies to adopting shared supply chain management practices that minimize waste and reduce carbon emissions.

For instance, consider a clothing retailer that partners with an environmentally responsible textile manufacturer. By working together, they can create garments made from sustainable materials, such as organic cotton or recycled polyester, thereby reducing the environmental footprint of their products. This partnership helps the retailer differentiate itself in the market and offers customers a more responsible choice at a price that reflects the added value and cost of sustainability.

Another example is the food industry, where some businesses

have collaborated with local farmers or cooperatives to source organic, ethically produced ingredients. This approach supports small-scale producers, promotes fair labor practices, and enables companies to provide customers with high-quality, sustainably sourced products at a premium price.

Using certifications and labels, along with strategic partnerships and collaborations, are key elements in successfully implementing sustainable pricing strategies. By embracing these tools and approaches, businesses can demonstrate their commitment to sustainability, attract environmentally conscious customers, and justify their pricing decisions, ultimately contributing to a more sustainable future.

Businesses must conduct a comprehensive sustainability assessment to implement sustainable pricing strategies effectively. This process involves examining the business's operations' environmental, social, and economic aspects to identify areas for improvement and opportunities for growth. By conducting such an assessment, companies can gain valuable insights into their current performance and develop a well-informed, strategic approach to sustainability.

One critical aspect of this assessment is setting measurable goals that align with the company's overall sustainability objectives. These goals should be ambitious and achievable, continually pushing the business to improve its practices while providing clear benchmarks for success. To track progress towards these goals, companies should establish key performance indicators (KPIs) that measure specific aspects of sustainability, such as energy consumption, waste reduction, or carbon emissions.

Regularly reviewing and evaluating these KPIs enables businesses to monitor their progress, make data-driven decisions, and adapt their strategies.

However, implementing sustainable pricing strategies has its challenges. One potential risk is greenwashing, a deceptive marketing practice in which a company promotes itself as environmentally responsible when its actual practices do not align with this image. To combat greenwashing, businesses should prioritize transparency and honesty in their communications, ensuring that concrete actions and verifiable data support their claims.

In addition, partnering with reputable certifications and organizations, as discussed in the previous scene, can further validate a company's commitment to sustainability.

Another challenge lies in the need for ongoing innovation and adaptation. As consumer preferences evolve and new technologies emerge, businesses must stay ahead of the curve to maintain their competitive edge in sustainable offerings. This requires a willingness to invest in research and development and a commitment to continuous learning and improvement. By fostering a culture of innovation, businesses can ensure the long-term success of their sustainable pricing strategies amidst a rapidly changing landscape.

In summary, conducting a thorough sustainability assessment and setting measurable goals are vital in developing and implementing effective, sustainable pricing strategies.

Businesses can mitigate risks by addressing challenges such as greenwashing and the need for ongoing innovation and maintaining their commitment to creating a more sustainable future.

The significance of integrating sustainability into pricing strategies cannot be overstated. To reiterate the key points discussed, businesses must first understand the concept of sustainability in terms of environmental, social, and economic considerations and acknowledge the growing consumer demand for eco-friendly products and services.

Recognizing the need to minimize their environmental impact, companies should explore various ways of incorporating sustainable practices into their pricing models, such as offering eco-friendly products or services at a premium price.

Additionally, examining practical examples and case studies offers invaluable insights into how other successful businesses have implemented sustainable pricing strategies.

Companies can learn from these organizations' challenges and emulate the positive outcomes they have achieved. Furthermore, embracing transparency and communication is vital in providing customers with a clear understanding of the environmental benefits of the products or services offered.

Incorporating certifications and labels that validate sustainable practices, such as organic or fair trade certifications, strengthens the credibility of a company's commitment to sustainability. Collaborations and partnerships with sustainable suppliers or organizations can further enhance a business's sustainability efforts, leading to a more robust and comprehensive approach to sustainable pricing.

To ensure long-term success, businesses must conduct a sustainability assessment, set measurable goals, and track progress. Addressing potential challenges and risks associated with sustainable pricing, such as greenwashing and the need for ongoing innovation and adaptation, is in maintaining a genuine commitment to a sustainable future.

With this knowledge, readers need to take action by assessing their own businesses' sustainability practices and considering implementing sustainable pricing strategies. For further reading on sustainable pricing in retail, consult reputable sources such as the Sustainable Packaging Coalition, the International Trade Centre, and the Ellen MacArthur Foundation, among others. By taking these steps, businesses can contribute to the greater good while bolstering their brand reputation and attracting environmentally conscious customers, ultimately paving the way for long-term success in the ever-evolving retail industry.

As we bring our focus on sustainable pricing strategies to a close, it is vital to recognize that this is just one aspect of mastering retail profit margins. The upcoming chapter will focus on another component for success in the retail industry: leveraging technology and data analytics to optimize pricing decisions.

In an era where technology is increasingly significant in shaping the retail landscape, businesses must stay informed and adapt their strategies accordingly. Embracing cutting-edge tools and techniques supports more effective decision-making and enables retailers to understand customer behavior, preferences, and trends better – all of which contribute to refining and enhancing pricing strategies.

The following chapter will explore how technology and data analytics can be harnessed to drive profitability while maintaining a strong commitment to sustainability. From harnessing artificial intelligence for dynamic pricing to utilizing big data for personalized promotions, the innovation potential is vast and exciting.

So, as we move forward, remember the importance of integrating sustainability into your pricing strategies while embracing the power of technology to maximize retail profit margins. The future of the retail industry lies at the intersection of these two critical areas, and mastering both will ensure a prosperous and enduring presence in the market.

Building Resilience and Protecting Margins

D iversifying revenue streams is one effective strategy for building resilience in retail businesses. By exploring various income-generating ways, retailers can mitigate risks associated with over reliance on a single product line or market segment. Diversification not only safeguards against fluctuations in demand but also provides the opportunity for growth and expansion into new areas of profitability.

For instance, expanding product lines is viable for retailers looking to diversify their revenue streams. Offering a more comprehensive range of products can attract a broader customer base and increase sales opportunities. For example, a retailer specializing in clothing might consider adding accessories or footwear to their inventory, thus appealing to customers interested in purchasing a complete outfit rather than just individual items.

Another approach for diversifying revenue streams involves entering new markets. Retailers should identify potential target markets and explore expansion opportunities, whether through opening physical stores, establishing an online presence, or both. This might include expanding into international markets, where there may be untapped demand for specific products or services. A local grocery store may launch an e-commerce platform to sell specialty items to customers beyond their immediate geographic area.

In summary, building resilience in retail businesses is essential for long-term success and protecting profit margins. Diversifying revenue streams through expanding product lines or entering new markets can help achieve this goal by mitigating risks and providing growth opportunities. Retailers must remain vigilant and adapt to changing market conditions to stay competitive and maintain a sustainable business model.

Beyond diversifying revenue streams, investing in employee training and development is another critical aspect of building resilience in retail businesses. A well-trained workforce enhances productivity and contributes to a positive work environment and customer satisfaction. By providing employees with the necessary skills and knowledge to perform their jobs effectively, retailers can ensure the overall success of their business.

Product-specific training sessions are one example of a training program that retailers can implement. These sessions familiarize employees with new products or services, allowing them to answer customer inquiries and provide valuable information confidently. For instance, an electronics retailer may hold training sessions on the latest gadgets and their features, enabling employees to keep up with technological advancements and assist customers in making informed purchase decisions.

In addition to product-specific training, retailers should consider offering employees professional development opportunities. This could include effective communication, sales techniques, and leadership skills workshops. By nurturing the growth of their workforce, retailers create a positive working environment that fosters collaboration and innovation – factors in maintaining a resilient business.

Alongside employee development, implementing robust financial planning is another essential aspect of building resilience in retail businesses. Retailers must regularly assess their financial health, set realistic goals, and adjust their strategies to optimize profit margins and maintain long-term stability.

To create an effective financial plan, retailers can conduct regular economic assessments examining key metrics such as revenue, expenses, and cash flow. A thorough analysis of these factors allows retailers to identify areas of improvement and make informed decisions about their business operations.

Setting realistic goals is also part of successful financial planning. Retailers must establish both short-term and long-term objectives that are achievable yet ambitious, taking into consideration factors such as market trends, competitive landscape, and available resources. For instance, a retailer might set a short-term goal of increasing sales by 10% over the next quarter, while their long-term goal could be to open a second store location within the next two years.

investing in employee training and development and implementing robust financial planning is to build resilience in retail businesses. Retailers can enhance productivity and customer satisfaction by equipping their employees with the necessary skills and knowledge. Moreover, by conducting regular financial assessments and setting realistic goals, they can optimize their profit margins and maintain long-term stability in an ever-changing market landscape.

To build resilience and protect profit margins, retailers must adopt specific strategies that focus on cost control, pricing optimization, and risk management. By implementing these tactics, businesses can enhance their profitability while maintaining a competitive edge in the market.

Cost control is an aspect of protecting profit margins in retail businesses. Retailers should explore various cost-saving measures, such as streamlining inventory management processes, reducing energy consumption, and renegotiating supplier contracts. For instance, implementing an efficient inventory management system can minimize stock discrepancies, prevent overstocking or understocking, and reduce warehouse costs. Similarly, investing in energy-efficient lighting and equipment can significantly lower energy bills and contribute to a greener environment.

Pricing optimization is another essential strategy for maximizing profit margins.

Retailers must regularly review and adjust their pricing strategies according to market fluctuations, consumer preferences, and competitor actions. This may involve adopting dynamic pricing models that allow real-time adjustments based on demand or utilizing data analytics to identify the optimal price points that maximize sales and profits. Retailers can optimize their pricing strategies to drive business growth by staying attuned to market trends and customer needs.

Risk management is vital in safeguarding profit margins by identifying potential threats and taking proactive measures to mitigate their impact. Retailers must conduct regular risk assessments, considering supply chain disruptions, cybersecurity vulnerabilities, and changing regulatory requirements. By establishing contingency plans and allocating resources accordingly, businesses can better navigate unpredictable circumstances and minimize potential losses.

In addition to these strategies, innovation, adaptability, and customer-centricity are fundamental factors contributing to achieving long-term success and building resilience in retail businesses. Embracing innovation allows retailers to stay ahead of the curve, capitalize on new opportunities, and differentiate themselves from competitors. This could include incorporating cutting-edge technology, such as artificial intelligence and virtual reality, into the shopping experience or developing unique product offerings that cater to niche markets.

Adaptability is another trait for retail businesses as the market landscape continuously evolves. Retailers must be agile and responsive to change, adapting their strategies and operations accordingly. This may involve pivoting their business model, embracing digital transformation, or exploring new distribution channels.

Moreover, customer-centricity lies at the heart of building resilience in retail businesses.

By prioritizing customer needs and expectations, retailers can cultivate strong relationships and foster loyalty among their clientele. This involves offering exceptional customer service, personalizing marketing efforts, and monitoring customer feedback to make informed improvements to products and services.

In summary, protecting profit margins and building resilience in retail businesses requires a multifaceted approach encompassing cost control, pricing optimization, risk management, innovation, adaptability, and customer-centricity. By adopting these strategies and remaining responsive to market changes, retailers can pave the way for long-term success in an increasingly competitive industry.

To illustrate the strategies' effectiveness further, let us examine a few case studies demonstrating how businesses have successfully implemented these approaches to build resilience and protect profit margins.

Case Study 1: A renowned fashion retailer embarked on a digital transformation journey, investing in e-commerce capabilities and leveraging data analytics to optimize product offerings. By diversifying their revenue streams and embracing innovation, the company navigated economic downturns and maintained a strong financial position. They also heavily emphasized customer-centricity, using data-driven insights to personalize marketing campaigns and enhance the shopping experience for their clientele.

Case Study 2: An independent bookstore faced stiff competition from larger chains and online retailers. To combat this challenge, they focused on building strong community ties by hosting local author events, offering personalized book recommendations, and supporting literacy programs. This customer-centric approach fostered loyalty among patrons and allowed the business to differentiate itself from competitors.

However, implementing these strategies has its challenges. Retailers may need more resources, resistance to change within the organization, or external factors like regulatory changes and supply chain disruptions.

To overcome these challenges, retailers must adopt a proactive mindset and be prepared to tackle potential roadblocks head-on. Here are some guidance on how to address common obstacles:

1. Limited resources: Allocate resources strategically by prioritizing initiatives with the highest impact and return on investment potential. Consider partnering with other organizations or seeking external funding to support your efforts.

2. Resistance to change: Foster a culture of adaptability and continuous learning within your organization. Communicate the benefits of the proposed changes and provide adequate support and training to help employees navigate the transition.

3. External factors: Stay abreast of industry trends and regulatory changes to anticipate potential challenges and develop contingency plans accordingly. Establish strong relationships with suppliers and partners to minimize the risk of supply chain disruptions.

Building resilience and protecting profit margins in retail businesses requires a strategic approach encompassing innovation, adaptability, customer-centricity, and effective risk management. By learning from the successes of others and anticipating potential challenges, retailers can implement these strategies effectively and set themselves up for long-term success.

As we delve deeper into strategies for building resilience in retail businesses, it is to address the importance of diversifying revenue streams. The key to adequate diversification lies in understanding your market and customer base while exploring new opportunities. Here are some practical tips that retailers can follow to achieve this goal:

1. Conduct thorough market research: Stay informed about industry trends and competitors' activities by analyzing relevant data and conducting surveys. This information will help you identify gaps in the market, tailor your product offerings, and make informed decisions about potential expansion.

2. Identify new target markets: Consider demographics, psychographics, and geographic factors when identifying potential customer segments. By catering to the specific needs and preferences of these new markets, retailers can unlock new sources of revenue.

3. Leverage existing customer relationships: Capitalize on your customer base by offering supplementary products or services, upselling, or cross-selling. Encourage customer loyalty through personalized offers and rewards programs, ensuring repeat business.

Now that we have explored strategies to diversify revenue streams let us focus on employee training and development. Investing in your workforce is essential for enhancing skill sets and fostering a culture of resilience within the organization. Here are some guidelines on how to design and implement effective training initiatives:

1. Identify training needs: Assess the current skill levels of your employees and determine areas where improvement is required. Align these needs with your organization's strategic goals and prioritize training initiatives accordingly.

2. Select appropriate training methods: Choose from various training methods, such as workshops, e-learning courses, or on-the-job training. Opt for a combination of techniques to accommodate different learning styles and ensure maximum engagement.

3. Evaluate the effectiveness of training initiatives: Regularly assess the impact of your training programs on employee performance and productivity. Use participant feedback and performance metrics to identify areas for improvement and adjust your approach as needed.

Diversifying revenue streams and investing in employee training are to build resilience in retail businesses. By implementing these strategies alongside effective financial planning, cost control measures, and a focus on innovation and adaptability, retailers can set the stage for long-term success in an ever-changing market landscape.

As we explore building resilience in retail businesses, it is vital to emphasize the importance of regularly reviewing and updating financial plans. Adapting to changing market conditions requires agility and responsiveness, ensuring the business can navigate the unpredictable tides of consumer behavior and economic fluctuations.

Monitoring key financial metrics is essential to maintain a firm grasp of your company's financial health. These may include cash flow, gross margin, inventory turnover, and return on investment.

Retailers should establish a robust system for tracking and analyzing these metrics to make informed financial decisions. This can be achieved by implementing financial management software, conducting regular economic assessments, and setting realistic goals based on the insights gleaned from the data. Engaging in scenario planning, evaluating the potential impact of various market changes on your business, and preparing contingency plans are .

In addition to sound financial management, effective communication and collaboration within the organization are pivotal in building resilience and protecting profit margins.

Fostering a culture of resilience and teamwork requires a concerted effort from all levels of the organization, starting with clear and transparent communication from leadership.

By articulating the company's vision, mission, and values, leaders can create a shared sense of purpose that unites employees in pursuing common goals.

One way to cultivate a resilient organizational culture is through regular team meetings, where employees can share their progress, challenges, and insights. Encourage open dialogue and active listening so each team member feels heard and valued. Additionally, consider providing opportunities for cross-functional collaboration, breaking down silos, and promoting a holistic understanding of the company's operations.

Another essential aspect of fostering teamwork is recognizing and celebrating individual and collective achievements. This can be done through employee recognition programs, performance bonuses, or simply acknowledging accomplishments during team meetings. By reinforcing the connection between hard work, collaboration, and success, you can inspire your team to strive for excellence and continuously adapt to change with resilience.

In summary, regularly reviewing and updating financial plans and fostering a culture of effective communication and collaboration is in building resilience within retail businesses. By monitoring key financial metrics, making informed decisions, and promoting teamwork, retailers can navigate the challenges of an ever-changing market landscape and secure long-term success.

In retail, assessing and managing risks is to build resilience and protect profit margins. A retailer must be constantly aware of potential threats to their business model, such as supply chain disruptions or changes in regulatory requirements, and take proactive steps to mitigate these risks.

To assess risks, retailers can start by conducting a thorough risk analysis. This process involves identifying potential hazards, evaluating their likelihood, and estimating the potential impact on the business. Typical risks retailers face include inventory obsolescence, theft or damage, supplier delays, and fluctuations in demand due to seasonal trends or economic factors. By understanding these risks, retailers can develop contingency plans and allocate resources accordingly, ensuring they are prepared for unforeseen circumstances.

For example, to manage the risk of supply chain disruptions, retailers can diversify their supplier base, opting for multiple suppliers for essential items rather than relying on a single source. This approach reduces dependency on any one supplier and ensures that the business has alternatives in case of any issues. Similarly, staying informed about changes in regulatory requirements allows retailers to anticipate and adapt to new rules, minimizing potential penalties and maintaining compliance.

Continuous monitoring and evaluation of implemented strategies are also of paramount importance. Retailers must track the effectiveness of their resilience-building efforts and make data-driven adjustments as needed. Key performance indicators (KPIs) can be used to measure the success of various initiatives, such as employee training programs, cost-saving measures, or the introduction of new revenue streams. By regularly reviewing these KPIs, retailers can identify areas of improvement and fine-tune their strategies to maximize efficiency and profitability.

Moreover, it is vital to maintain a close connection between strategic planning and day-to-day operations. Retailers should ensure that their long-term objectives are reflected in the actions of their team members, aligning the entire organization towards the goal of building resilience and protecting profit margins. This alignment can be achieved through regular communication, goal-setting, and performance evaluations.

Retailers must proactively identify, assess, and manage risks that may impact their profit margins. They can build resilience and ensure long-term success in the ever-evolving retail landscape by continuously monitoring the effectiveness of implemented strategies and making informed adjustments as needed.

In the retail industry, building resilience is critical for achieving long-term success and safeguarding profit margins. As we have discussed throughout this chapter, retailers can employ several key strategies to enhance their resilience and maintain a competitive edge in an ever-changing marketplace.

Diversifying revenue streams is an essential aspect of this

process, enabling businesses to mitigate risks associated with overreliance on a single source of income. Retailers can explore various avenues to diversify their revenue streams, such as expanding product lines, entering new markets, or leveraging existing customer relationships.

Investing in employee training and development programs is another strategy for fostering resilience. By enhancing the skills and knowledge of their workforce, retailers can improve operational efficiency, reduce employee turnover, and create a more agile organization capable of responding effectively to changing market conditions.

Robust financial planning underpins all efforts to build resilience and protect profit margins. Retailers should conduct regular economic assessments, set realistic goals, and monitor key financial metrics to make informed decisions. This approach enables businesses to identify potential challenges and adapt their strategies accordingly.

Protecting profit margins requires a multifaceted approach, encompassing cost control, pricing optimization, and risk management. Retailers must proactively identify and implement cost-saving measures while regularly reviewing and adjusting pricing strategies to ensure competitiveness and profitability.

Innovation, adaptability, and customer-centricity play a vital role in building resilience.

Retailers prioritizing these factors will be better equipped to navigate shifting market dynamics and capitalize on emerging opportunities.

Throughout this chapter, we have provided case studies and examples of businesses that have successfully implemented these strategies. These examples serve as valuable guidance for other retailers seeking to build resilience within their organizations. It's important to note that challenges and obstacles may arise while implementing these strategies, but with perseverance, adaptability, and a strong focus on the end goal, retailers can overcome these hurdles and emerge stronger.

In summary, building resilience is an ongoing process that requires retailers to adopt a proactive and strategic approach. By incorporating the critical strategies discussed in this chapter - diversifying revenue streams, investing in employee training and development, implementing robust financial planning, protecting profit margins, and fostering innovation, adaptability, and customer-centricity - retailers will be well-positioned for long-term success in their industry.

Conclusion

As we commence this chapter, revisiting and consolidating the key concepts, strategies, and insights presented throughout the book is . The cornerstone of success in the retail industry lies in understanding and effectively managing profit margins. By grasping these essential principles, retailers can unlock their true potential and reap the benefits of a thriving business.

Each chapter has provided valuable takeaways, designed with practicality and applicability. These strategies can significantly impact retail establishments' growth and profitability when employed correctly. Let us reiterate the main points from each chapter to ensure a comprehensive understanding of these vital techniques.

In the first chapter, we explored the fundamentals of retail economics, emphasizing the importance of revenue generation, cost control, and profitability management. This foundation allowed us to delve deeper into specific strategies in subsequent chapters.

Chapter two focused on understanding customer behavior and

purchasing patterns. The ability to anticipate and adapt to consumer preferences is pivotal for maximizing sales and profit margins.

Next, in chapter three, we examined various pricing strategies and their impact on revenue and customer satisfaction. By employing dynamic pricing, psychological pricing, and other methods, retailers can optimize their pricing structures to serve their target markets better.

The fourth chapter discussed inventory management and its role in achieving optimal profit margins. Efficient stock control and product turnover are essential for minimizing costs associated with excess or obsolete inventory, thereby improving overall profitability.

The fifth chapter dealt with the significance of merchandising and product presentation in driving sales. A visually appealing and strategically organized store layout can significantly influence customer purchases and encourage higher spending.

Finally, in chapter six, we discussed the importance of leveraging data analytics and technology to make informed pricing, inventory management, and customer engagement decisions. Harnessing the power of big data allows retailers to stay ahead of the competition and maximize their profit margins.

By reviewing and internalizing these key takeaways, retailers can enhance their understanding and mastery of profit margins in the retail industry. Armed with this knowledge, they can embark on a journey towards sustainable growth and success.

Consider the remarkable success story of a small, family-owned retail store that managed to triple its profit margins within just a few years. The owners transformed their business into a thriving and prosperous enterprise by implementing the strategies discussed throughout this book. They started by reassessing their pricing and inventory management systems, making data-driven decisions that improved product turnover and reduced costs associated with excess stock. Additionally, they revamped their store layout and merchandising techniques, creating an inviting and stimulating shopping environment for their customers.

This real-world example demonstrates the power and relevance of the concepts we've explored in the retail landscape. Retailers must take these lessons to heart and apply them to their businesses. By doing so, they can unlock their full potential and significantly improve profitability.

Now is the perfect time for you, the reader, to pause and reflect on your retail business.

Ask yourself: How can I effectively implement these strategies to enhance my profit margins? What aspects of my current operations require improvement or innovation? Consider each method, from pricing to inventory management, merchandising, and leveraging data analytics. Identify areas where you have room for growth and devise a concrete plan to address these opportunities.

On this journey, remember that mastering profit margins is an ongoing process. The retail industry continually evolves, and business owners must stay adaptable and open-minded. Embrace change, learn from your experiences, and continue refining your approach.

The path to success in the retail industry lies in understanding and mastering profit margins. By applying the strategies discussed throughout this book, retailers can significantly improve their profitability and lay the foundation for sustainable growth. With dedication and resilience, there is no limit to what can be achieved in this dynamic and rewarding sector.

The ever-evolving retail landscape requires continuous learning and improvement. As the sun rises and sets, so does the industry shift with new trends and innovations, much like the changing colors of a chameleon. To master profit margins, you must stay informed about these trends and constantly seek new ways to elevate your business as a retailer.

Imagine standing at the edge of an ocean, where the waves represent the constant flow of information in the retail industry. It can be overwhelming, but embracing the tides of change will allow you to stay ahead and adapt effectively. To achieve this, you must actively pursue knowledge and remain curious about the developments within the sector, ensuring that your business remains competitive and profitable.

One way to stay informed is through industry publications. These resources contain valuable insights into the latest retail trends, groundbreaking research, and expert opinions. By subscribing to reputable journals or magazines, such as the Harvard Business Review or Retail Dive, you ensure a steady stream of pertinent information reaches your hands, equipping you with the tools to make informed decisions for your business.

Another avenue for continued learning is online courses. Platforms like Coursera, LinkedIn Learning, and Udemy offer a wide range of retail-focused classes covering pricing strategies, inventory management, and customer service. Through these virtual classrooms, you can expand your knowledge and sharpen your skills at your own pace, enabling you to implement cutting-edge practices and continually improve your profit margins.

Relevant conferences also provide opportunities for networking and knowledge-sharing.

You can connect with industry leaders by attending events such as the National Retail Federation's annual convention or the ShopTalk Retail Conference and learn from their experiences. The collective wisdom at these gatherings can inspire new ideas and approaches to enhance your business's profitability.

As a retailer navigating the vast sea of industry changes, remember that continuous learning and improvement are vital to mastering profit margins. Your business will survive and thrive in the dynamic retail landscape by staying informed through various resources and actively seeking new ways to grow.

The potential for growth and success from mastering profit margins is genuinely remarkable. As a retailer, investing time and effort into understanding and implementing the strategies discussed in this book can significantly benefit your business. Through these methods, you can unlock new expansion opportunities, attract and retain loyal customers, and ultimately achieve long-lasting financial stability.

Visualize your retail store operating at peak efficiency with optimized inventory levels, streamlined processes, and an engaged workforce focused on delivering exceptional customer experiences. This vision is achievable when you apply the principles of profit margin mastery. By taking action and incorporating these strategies into your day-to-day operations, you can transform your business into a thriving enterprise poised to capitalize on emerging market trends.

However, it is essential to remember that the retail landscape is ever-changing, with shifting consumer preferences and technological advancements continually reshaping the industry. Adapting to these changes and staying ahead of emerging trends is critical to protecting profit margins. Resilience is your greatest ally in the face of fluctuating market conditions – the ability to adapt and innovate will help your business weather any storm.

As you implement the various strategies presented in this book, keep a watchful eye on the horizon for new developments that may impact your retail business. By staying informed and responsive to change, you can pivot your strategy as needed, ensuring that your profit margins remain protected even as the winds of industry shift.

Mastering profit margins requires dedication, continuous learning, and adaptability. The fruits of your labor will be a robust, thriving, and resilient retail business capable of navigating the challenges of an ever-evolving industry. Embrace the journey and seize the opportunity to unlock your potential as a successful retailer.

In today's retail landscape, sustainability is an ethical consideration and a key factor influencing pricing strategies. Consumers are becoming more environmentally conscious, and businesses that incorporate sustainable practices into their models can reap the benefits of this shift in consumer preferences. As a retailer, recognizing the impact of sustainability on your pricing strategies is to maintain a competitive edge in the market.

To effectively incorporate sustainable practices into your business model, consider evaluating your supply chain, product sourcing, and packaging materials. Making thoughtful choices in these areas can lead to cost savings, increased customer satisfaction, and higher profit margins. By embracing sustainability, you demonstrate your commitment to the environment and the well-being of future generations, which can resonate with customers and enhance brand loyalty.

Let us revisit the critical strategies for increasing profit margins discussed throughout the book. These strategies include:

1. Cost optimization: Analyze and minimize expenses across all aspects of your business, from inventory management to marketing efforts, and pass those savings on to your customers through competitive pricing.

2. Upselling and cross-selling: Train your staff to promote complementary or higher-value products to customers effectively, boosting sales volume and average transaction value.

3. Diversifying product lines: Expand your offerings to cater to different customer segments while carefully managing inventory levels to avoid overstock and obsolescence.

These strategies and sustainable practices form the foundation for a successful retail business with healthy profit margins. Reflect on how these approaches may be relevant to your retail operation, and consider how to implement them to drive growth and success.

As a retailer, adopting a proactive mindset and focusing on continuous improvement will help you stay ahead in the ever-evolving retail industry. By mastering profit margins through strategic pricing, sustainable practices, and a deep understanding of your customer base, you can unlock the full potential of your retail business and secure lasting success.

In addition to the strategies detailed earlier, retailers must maintain an ethical approach to pricing. A transparent and fair pricing structure not only fosters trust but also helps in building lasting customer loyalty. As a retailer, your commitment should be to maximizing profits and upholding the highest standards of integrity and honesty in all aspects of your business.

Consider, for instance, the practice of dynamic pricing. While this strategy can boost profit margins by adjusting prices based on demand, supply, or market conditions, ensuring that these adjustments are reasonable and communicated to customers is . This transparency will create a sense of fairness, strengthening the bond between you and your clientele.

Similarly, when offering promotional discounts or limited-time offers, please ensure that the original prices remain visible so that customers can easily discern the savings they receive. By being upfront about pricing policies and ensuring that customers feel well-informed, you demonstrate your dedication to their best interests and earn their trust over time.

As we conclude this chapter, remember that mastering profit margins in the retail industry requires continuous learning and adaptation. Stay informed about the latest trends, technologies, and practices to ensure your business remains agile and innovative in the face of ever-evolving market conditions. In doing so, you secure your success and contribute to the retail industry's overall growth and vitality.

Let this book serve as a beacon, guiding you toward realizing your full potential as a retail entrepreneur. Embrace the strategies outlined herein, always mindful of the ethical implications, and continue to seek new ways to optimize your business operations while delivering exceptional value to your customers. Through this unwavering pursuit of excellence, you will find enduring success, carving out a legacy of which you can be proud.

Take heart and venture forth confidently, knowing that the keys to mastering profit margins and achieving greatness lie within your grasp. On this exciting journey, may you be ever mindful of your responsibilities as a retailer and always strive to positively impact your customers, your employees, and the world at large.

Resources

While mastering retail profit margins does require dedication, retailers need not go it alone. A wealth of software tools and professional services are available to provide invaluable assistance.

Pricing Optimization Software

Rather than relying on guesswork, retailers can utilize advanced pricing software to maximize profits. Solutions like Pricefx, Zilliant, and KBMax employ sophisticated algorithms to recommend optimal prices aligned to business goals. Intuitive interfaces make these tools accessible even for pricing teams with limited expertise. By automating analytics, they empower strategic decisions.

Customer Data Platforms

Understanding customers is the key to maximizing margins. Customer data platforms (CDPs) like Salesforce CDP, Adobe Real-Time CDP, and Segment CDP capture granular data from all customer touchpoints. This enables precise segmentation for tailored pricing strategies and targeted promotions.

Inventory Management Software

Monitoring inventory performance is easier than ever with cloud-based software solutions. Market leaders such as TradeGecko, Cin7, and Brightpearl provide end-to-end inventory visibility from ordering to sales. Built-in analytics spotlight fast/slow-moving items, reduce stockouts, and optimize turnover.

Customer Relationship Management (CRM) Software
- Salesforce
- HubSpot
- Shopify

By implementing these software tools, retailers can automate many complex tasks associated with pricing strategies, inventory control, and understanding customer data to enhance decision making and boost profitability.

Professional Services

For retailers preferring hands-on guidance, consulting firms like The Retail Concepts Company offer personalized advice for building pricing models and promotional strategies. While software provides the heavy number crunching, the human touch addresses nuanced business needs. With flexible and affordable packages, the ROI is compelling.

Suggested Educational Resources

Websites

- National Retail Federation (nrf.com)
- Retail Wire (retailwire.com)
- Retail Dive (retaildive.com)

Online Courses
- Profitability Analysis in Retail Fundamentals (Coursera)
- Retail Analytics (Udemy)
- Prices and Promotions Management (edX)

Publications
- Harvard Business Review (hbr.org)
- Journal of Retailing (journals.elsevier.com/journal-of-retailing)
- MIT Sloan Management Review (sloanreview.mit.edu)

Through a blended approach of employing cutting-edge retail tech while also accessing specialized expertise, retailers can make significant strides towards profit margin mastery and elevated success, unencumbered by resource constraints. The tools exist to turn aspiration into achievement. Now is the time to leverage these capabilities and unlock your potential.

Index

A

Automation, 135-136
Average transaction value, 98-100

B

Big data, 127-128
Bundling products, 99

C

Calculating margins, 77-85
Case studies, 56, 66, 77, 98, 113
Certifications, 148-149
Channels, marketing, 94
Competitor pricing analysis, 73, 91
Consumer behavior, 34
Controlling costs, 104, 119-121
Cross-selling, 98-99
Customer experience, 29

Customer loyalty, 97, 132
Customer segmentation, 93

D

Data analytics, 55, 113
    Data collection, 50–51
    Demand forecasting, 107, 121–122
    Digital transformation, 115
    Direct costs, 38
    Discounts, 100
    Diversifying product lines, 97, 132
    Diversifying revenue streams, 113–114
    Dynamic pricing, 74, 91, 128

E

E-commerce trends, 28
    Economic fluctuations, 103–106, 119–122
    Employee development, 114
    Environmental impact, 141
    Ethical pricing practices, 87–90
    Expenses, reducing, 96

F

Financial planning, 114–115

G

Global supply chains, 125–134

Gross profit margin, 77-81

H

High-volume pricing, 72-73

I

Inflation, adjusting prices during, 105
   Innovation, adapting through, 115
   Inventory management, 23, 55, 107, 122-123
   Inventory turnover, 130

J

Just-in-time inventory, 121

K

Key performance indicators (KPIs), 130

L

Labor costs, 40-41, 105
   Logistics optimization, 133

M

Margins, importance of, 9
   Marketing channels, 94
   Merchandising, 56

N

Natural disasters, supply chain, 125
  Net profit margin, 81–85
  New markets, entering, 113

O

Omnichannel retailing, 28, 135
  Online reputation management, 129–130
  Overhead expenses, 43–45

P

Partnerships, sustainability-focused, 149
  Performance evaluation, 115
  Personalization, 136
  Premium pricing, 73
  Pricing psychology, 87–88
  Pricing transparency, 88–90
  Pricing strategies by product type, 75
  Procurement costs, lowering, 120

Product costing, 37–42
  Product lines, diversifying, 97, 132
  Professional services, outsourcing, 46
  Promoting positive reviews, 131
  Psychological pricing tactics, 88

Q

Quality inspections, 123

R

Raw material costs, 40-41
   Reference pricing, 90
   Regulations and legal compliance, 111-118
   Research methods, market, 136-137
   Resources and courses for further learning, 68, 134
   Retail technologies, 55, 97
   Returns processing, optimizing, 123
   Revenue growth opportunities, identifying, 137

S

Sales volume analysis, 50
   Scenario planning, financial, 115
   Seasonal inventory planning, 56
   Segmenting customers, 93
   Self-checkout technologies, 135
   SKU rationalization, 123
   Social responsibility trends, 141
   Software solutions for pricing and inventory optimization, 46, 55
   Staffing level optimization, 123
   Staying informed, industry changes, 111-112
   Stock keeping unit (SKU) analysis, 51
   Sustainability trends, 29, 135, 141-150
   Sustainable materials, sourcing, 143

T

Target markets, expanding into new, 113
    Tariffs on imported goods, 112, 117
    Taxes, impact of changing, 112
    Technologies, retail, 55, 97
    Tiered pricing plans, 92
    Training employees, 114
    Transparency in pricing, 87-90
    Trend analysis, 50

U

Upselling products or services, 98-99

V

Value propositions, tailoring to, 71
    Visibility, supply chain, 133

W

Warehouse management optimization, 123
    Waste reduction, 143